DAT

J.D. Salinger

ALSO BY THOMAS BELLER

Seduction Theory: Stories

The Sleep-Over Artist: A Novel

How to Be a Man: Scenes from a Protracted Boyhood

J.D. Salinger

THE ESCAPE ARTIST

THOMAS BELLER

ICONS SERIES

New Harvest
Houghton Mifflin Harcourt
BOSTON • NEW YORK

www.hmhco.com

Library of Congress Cataloging-in-Publication Data
Beller, Thomas, author.
J.D. Salinger : the escape artist / Thomas Beller.
pages cm. — (Icons)
ISBN 978-0-544-26199-0 (hardback)
1. Salinger, J. D. (Jerome David), 1919–2010. 2. Authors,
American — 20th century — Biography. I. Title.
PS3537.A426Z565 2014
813.54 — dc23
[B]
2013045583

Book design by Brian Moore

Printed in the United States of America
DOC 10 9 8 7 6 5 4 3 2

For Elizabeth

Contents

1923: On Running Away

I N 1923, when J.D. Salinger was four years old, his mother went out shopping and left him in the care of his sister, Doris, who was ten. Sonny, as his family called him, was extremely close to his sister. They spent a lot of time together. She often took him to the movies. Doris Salinger describes the experience: "In those days, you know, the movies were silent and had subtitles that I had to read to him out loud. Boy, he wouldn't let you miss a single one. The rows used to empty out all around us!"

Immediately one feels a moment of recognition, the aural version of a double take. There is no one like the grown-up Doris Salinger in J.D. Salinger's fiction — a successful career woman, twice divorced, a buyer for Bloomingdale's most fashionable department, moving amid other strong, well-earning ladies in New York City's garment and fashion world — and yet something about that voice, its wised-up, exclamatory energy combined with a note of exasperation, sounds familiar.

On the day in question, when their mother was out shopping and left them alone, the siblings had a fight. "I forget about what," Doris would say almost sixty years later. The cause of the fight is forgotten but not the result. Sonny packed a suitcase, dressed himself in his Indian outfit, and left the apartment. He didn't leave the building, though. A couple of hours later, his mother arrived in the lobby and found her son, dressed head to toe in his Indian costume, complete with a long feather head-dress. His suitcase was by his side. "Mother, I'm running away," he said. "But I stayed to say goodbye to you."

They went upstairs and opened the suitcase. It was full of toy soldiers.

The Gift

S HORTLY AFTER I decided to write a biography of J.D.
Salinger, I went to the home of a man who was in posses-
sion of an invaluable bit of evidence. He lived on West
Seventy-Seventh Street, across the street from the American
Museum of Natural History.

When I was a little kid I would come to this block every
year. A childhood friend lived up the street, and on the night
before Thanksgiving his family would have a party. We would
watch the Thanksgiving Day parade floats get inflated. Later I
became aware that Philip Roth had an apartment on this block,
and I associated it with him. I would see Roth now and then in
the neighborhood and once stood next to him in line at Osner
Business Machines, a typewriter shop on Amsterdam Avenue
that lasted well into the personal computer age. I remember
thinking it seemed significant that Roth, waiting in line on the
worn linoleum floor, still used a typewriter. But now the street
would take on a new dimension and association that should
have been there all along: J.D. Salinger used the Museum of
Natural History as a setting for *The Catcher in the Rye*. Holden
recalling his school trip to the museum. The titillation of the
bare breast in one of the dioramas.

My host greeted me warmly and led me into the living room,
where I encountered the roof of the Museum of Natural History and a lot of sky. There was a divan or a chaise longue — I'm

not sure which is the right term — and other comfortable, over-stuffed pieces of furniture. The light was glorious.

He had to go do something before he could sit down with me, and so I had the experience of being alone in a strange house with the prerogative to poke around and explore. This certainly did not involve stealing anything, or even touching anything. But it did allow for a level of scrutiny beyond what one would feel comfortable doing in the presence of another person. I got to my feet and walked around. Mostly I stared at the books. Many, many interesting books. Among them biographies of Delmore Schwartz and Saul Bellow.

Schwartz and Bellow. A bit of an echo there. Literary Jews. They were both from elsewhere — Brooklyn and Chicago, re-spectively — but had done time on Manhattan's Upper West Side, probably somewhere north of the Museum of Natural History. Schwartz grew up in Washington Heights; Bellow set one of his major novels, *Mr. Sammler's Planet,* on the Up-per West Side. A line that I seem to remember from Bellow's *Humboldt's Gift* (not that I could ever find it) flickered in my mind — the protagonist, I recalled, was a professor who could barely keep himself together in any of the normal ways but could discuss bird imagery in Dante with the dean. A genius who can't tie his shoelaces, in other words, which is more or less how Margaret Salinger characterized her father in her memoir, *Dream Catcher.*

My host returned, and we settled in for a nice chat. At some point he handed me, in a mode that for some reason I associ-ated with a Bar Mitzvah gift, a bound galley of Ian Hamilton's *J.D. Salinger: A Writing Life.*

"I think you'll find this useful," he said. "It's very rare." I took it in my hands.

I had heard about Ian Hamilton's biography and its peculiar fate, but I had no sense of the world as those events unfolded.

Only with time did I start to understand what a profoundly strange spectacle the whole thing was. Everyone who cared about book publishing was familiar with the case. Everyone who cared about, or had participated in, biography or biographical research knew about it. It was appealed all the way to the Supreme Court. The case "has hung like a rain cloud over the head of every biographer since," in the words of D.T. Max, David Foster Wallace's biographer.

Hamilton was British. His handwriting, I would soon learn, was fastidious and minute. He had produced, prior to embarking on his Salinger project, a biography of the poet Robert Lowell, which involved his becoming embroiled with all manner of dysfunctional American aristocracy — Boston society stretching back to the *Mayflower,* money, Harvard, WASP rectitude, and the other side of that coin, the spectacle of nervous breakdowns in public.

Salinger, a grandson of immigrants and half Jewish (but learning of the half that was not Jewish quite late), came from a milieu that couldn't have been more different from Lowell's, although there are some similarities: both men were iconic figures of postwar American literature. Lowell was a total insider who was nevertheless insane — out of his own mind — or on the verge of becoming so, for much of his life; Salinger was a consummate outsider who made sanity, and what the definition of it might be, the prevailing theme of his later fiction, and who lived for more than half of his ninety-one years in a seclusion that held within it an intense ambiguity, one could almost say a riddle, that riveted a portion of the American, and global, public. This raised a question: Was his seclusion, his allergy to publicity, his self-silencing to the point of refusing to publish, evidence that he had gone crazy? Or did his choices about how to live — about which he proselytized hardly at all outside of his fiction — amount to a kind of judgment on everyone else? Salinger's narrators are preoccupied with matters of authenticity—Holden Caulfield is probably famous above all else for calling everyone a phony—but his writings are first and foremost stories. Their purpose is in their form; they are not disguised pieces of propaganda, political, religious, or philosophical. But they nevertheless function as a kind of litmus test by which readers can measure their own lives and values.

Autobiography is woven into the work of both Lowell and Salinger. Writing about them is therefore by necessity a kind of a puzzle for a biographer. This is true of every biography but especially true of those of authors whose art is strewn with clues, like eggs at an Easter egg hunt, or its seasonal parallel, the search for the Afikoman at the Passover Seder.

Hamilton's biography of Robert Lowell was authorized, a doorstopper of a book brimming with facts, voices, quoted letters. To read even a few chapters is to grasp that its composition was an act of omission, weeding out and narrowing down. The Salinger project would demand an entirely different set of instincts and reflexes. It would be an act of gathering together little scraps and trying to make a mosaic. Of trying to find a form. A kind of literary forensic work; except unlike with Lowell, the body under examination wasn't merely warm. It was alive and kicking.

Armed with a contract from Random House, Hamilton began writing letters to every Salinger in the New York City telephone book, announcing his project and asking if he or she was related to the author. He sent one to J.D. Salinger himself, saying that he was undertaking a biography. His language was respectful even if his intent was not. He wasn't writing Salinger with the expectation of getting cooperation or permission. It was a nod to good manners. He explained that his book would concern itself only with the years that Salinger was a working writer, and therefore a public figure. It would stop in 1965, when Salinger published his last story.

Hamilton's letter strikes a faintly chivalric note, like one gentleman wishing another good luck before they both march off ten paces and turn to shoot each other. He knew what he was getting into — or he thought he did. The Salinger project would be the opposite of the Lowell.

Just as wars are declared with a shot, biographies are declared with a letter.

Salinger's response was artful, direct, angry, charming. It begins by expressing contempt for this intruder; but it is not outright nasty contempt; there is a rueful quality to it, and it almost feels as though what Salinger is ruing isn't just our insatiable appetite for gossip and cheap literary thrills but his own compulsive habit of being charming in letters. By the end, though, he is full of self-pity, evoking intrusions onto his private physical and mental landscape that have taxed him beyond his emotional means. Salinger had endured a prolonged war with woodchucks on his New Hampshire property; he had built fences, he had worked to eradicate them in any number of ways. But he had more affection for the woodchucks, one feels, than he had for Hamilton.

Salinger's letter, though a bit melodramatic, is also a centered, rational expression of his anger and contempt, while making a gesture, futile but necessary, toward persuading Hamilton to go away. Throughout his life, Salinger's letters didn't just open a window onto his life; they were occasions for Salinger to practice the one thing he was really good at, which was being himself.

Hamilton went ahead with his biography anyway. The book he produced, *J.D. Salinger: A Writing Life,* was filled with quotations from Salinger's personal correspondence with Elizabeth Murray and Whit Burnett, two formative figures in Salinger's life with whom he corresponded for decades. His letters to them were, in a way, like a diary, a continuous thread. As soon as Salinger learned about the book and its quotations he sued to stop it from being published. His argument was that regardless of who owned the physical letters, the words still belonged to him. *Salinger v. Random House* went two rounds. The publisher won the first. Salinger appealed and won the second in a knockout. The case was appealed to the Supreme Court, which refused to hear it.

Hamilton had to go back to his desk and start over, excising all the quoted letters. A new book, *In Search of J.D. Salinger,* was eventually published. That it was vastly inferior to *J.D. Salinger: A Writing Life* was due largely to the absence of J.D. Salinger's voice. But it didn't help that in the new book Hamilton used a conceit in which he splits himself into two characters, one "grappling feebly with the moral issues" of writing a book against its subject's wishes, the other his "biographizing alter ego," who has no such misgivings. Hamilton's astute critical intelligence — which found its most vivid expression in his ability to extract and highlight the telling line in a piece of writing — was replaced by a forced grin. Mostly *In Search of J.D. Salinger* reads like a eulogy for *J.D. Salinger: A Writing Life,* the book that was now in my possession.

The trial was widely covered in newspapers and magazines at the time. Its immediate, sensational effect was to put into the public record the very thing Hamilton's biography most conspicuously lacked, namely, an interview with J.D. Salinger. The exchange between Salinger and Robert Callagy, counsel for the defense, at times resembles a *Paris Review* interview:

CALLAGY: Have you written a full-length work of fiction in the last twenty years?

SALINGER: What do you mean by "full-length work"? You mean ready for publication?

CALLAGY: As opposed to a short story or a fictional piece or a magazine submission.[1]

SALINGER: I don't write that way. I just start writing fiction and see what happens to it.

Everyone had been wondering what he had been doing in New Hampshire for the twenty-odd years since he'd last been published. What he had been doing, he said on the witness stand and under oath, was writing.

Anyone interested in Salinger's work, then and now, can't help being slapped by the irony of the whole predicament. There probably isn't another writer who has invested more energy in making letters, the actual, physical things, so central to the action of his stories and plots. It almost seems as if every other story involves someone fishing a letter out of his or her pocket. Lane Coutell waiting for Franny on the train platform; Zooey Glass sitting in his bathtub, delicately handling a four-year-old letter while simultaneously smoking and talking to his mother.[2]

---

1 I take it back: No *Paris Review* interviewer would be so obtuse as to ask one of the most celebrated short story writers of the second half of the century — the guy who once declared, "I'm a dash man, not a miler" — "Is it a fully realized work of fiction or is it just a short story or some fiction for a magazine?" On the other hand, Callagy is asking a question that any reader of "Zooey," or "Seymour: An Introduction," or "Hapworth 16, 1924," might have spoken aloud to the page as they read: "What is this supposed to be?"

2 Letters, or packages, appear so often in Salinger's fiction that his need to insert them is almost a form of narrative addiction. "A Boy in France," one of the gems of his early, uncollected work, is a rare depiction of a character in battlefield conditions. But when the boy is finally situated in his foxhole, he pulls a pair of letters from his pocket and enters that cloistered mental space of the letter reader. Salinger's characters escape into their letters as though they were portals in time, little respites from the grueling present, whether that present is a bathtub in a Park Avenue apartment or a foxhole in France. They are not read

As communication, as metaphor, as talisman, as literary calisthenics, letters were central to J.D. Salinger's life and imagination, and now they, or the people he had written to, had apparently betrayed him.

When Hamilton and Random House were first confronted with Salinger's strenuous objections to having any of his letters included in the book, they revised it to include far fewer excerpts. A second set of galley proofs was printed. At the trial there were references to the "May galleys" and the "October galleys."

Salinger won the case. As a result nobody saw *J.D. Salinger: A Writing Life,* either the May or October versions. Or almost nobody. Some of the May galleys had been sent out into the world. One of them was now in my possession.

The matte paper cover was the muted color of a lemon drop. Onto this had been pasted a white sheet with informational text — title, author, publisher, and publication date: August 29, 1986. At the top of this sheet, in large letters, were the words ADVANCE PROOFS. The *n* and *c* of "advance" had been encircled in a coffee stain, in a way that I found kind of stylish, as if it were part of the design. The whole book, while in good enough shape, nevertheless looked a bit tattered and fragile. I stood to leave with the book in my hand. My host wished me well, and sent me off with his good wishes and his treasure.

"Don't lose it," he said, half kidding. Maybe less than half.

---

and discarded but read, and refolded, and quite often shoved into a pocket.

3

Lost

I WANDER OUT INTO early evening on Seventy-Seventh Street and bike ten blocks home, where I put the book in a special place. But it's not quite right to use the word "home." I bike to my mother's apartment, where I grew up, and where my family and I now camp out for extended stays when visiting New York.

It is summer. Summers used to last longer, I feel. Now I hardly get to the halfway point before it starts to feel like I am getting ready to decamp back to New Orleans, where I teach at Tulane University. But that evening, with my newly won prize, I feel there is time. Time to savor the city. Time to contemplate Salinger. Time to read the book in which J.D. Salinger's pilfered words, which he had written in the late 1930s, 1940s, and beyond, with every expectation that they would be seen by their recipient alone, were now available to me. The book was by Ian Hamilton, but the anticipated pleasure was reading J.D. Salinger.[1]

———

---

1 You can read these letters in their entirety, as I eventually did, by going to Princeton or writing to the University of Texas at Austin, but I was attached to the idea of Hamilton's book being the delivery vehicle; a biography of Salinger, even one undertaken after his death, cannot help feeling like a theft of some kind, and I figured the only way I could transcend the guilt that attended this atmosphere was to embrace it.

A week goes by. Then another. Then another. That Hamilton galley blinks out at me from its special place. I don't read it. But I take comfort in knowing where it is. My family and I make the move to New Orleans, and eventually, when we are unpacked, it occurs to me that I haven't seen that lemon-drop-yellow book in a while. A search ensues. I assume it is at my mother's. But when I next visit New York it is not in the special place. I have a dim recollection of moving it from the special place to an even more special place. I search for it, but it is in no place. I have lost the book.

I am totally stricken at my inability to locate my galley of Ian Hamilton's *J.D. Salinger: A Writing Life.* This is not wildly out of character for me. I almost turned it down when its owner held it toward me so lovingly, a tattered and delicate thing.

Almost immediately, once the full panic sets in, I am confronted with the metaphor of the circumstance. In so much of Salinger's work there is a nearly pathological emphasis on privacy. I do not mean the famous, hermetic privacy to which the man retreated in life, but rather the sense of privacy that permeates the fiction. Really, I thought, trying to calm myself about the loss of *J.D. Salinger: A Writing Life,* it's impossible even to contemplate writing a biography of Salinger without getting into the issues of privacy, secrecy, intimacy, and, by extension, betrayal. To read this suppressed book would be a theft.

But, I thought, surely the author's death changes things. The change is legal, physical, and moral. It involves permission — that which you must acquire and that which you can, in good conscience, grant yourself. In some ways, this basic fact — that death changes things — is the burning ember that sits at the center of Salinger's fiction. I suppose this book can be framed as, among other things, a quest to find out why this is the case. That the process might involve thrusting my hand into a coat pocket and yanking out a letter is unpleasant to contemplate. I have to remind myself that the owner's hand is no longer there. The hand, literally Salinger's hand, is gone. But the letters, the fiction, the voice, and the curiosity to know how that voice came into being remain.

4

1930s: Ham and Cheese

J.D. SALINGER GREW up thinking he had a Jewish mother named Miriam, when in fact his mother was not Jewish, or named Miriam. His father, Solomon, was Jewish and in the ham and cheese business. He downplayed the ham.

Miriam had once been Marjorie. The name change was to appease Solomon's parents, especially his father, Simon, a Russian immigrant who had financed his medical school education by practicing as a rabbi in Louisville, Kentucky, of all places, before getting his degree. Then he moved his family to Chicago, where Solomon grew up.

Miriam grew up in Iowa. She never formally converted to Judaism beyond the name change — her father passed away during the period of her courtship with Sol, when she was seventeen. Her mother moved away with her youngest sister; it was as though she had graduated from her family and then it vanished before she even had a chance to be nostalgic for it. The refuge of family was now her fiancé — and his family. The act of changing her name to appease her in-laws is touched not just with romance but with expediency.

After they were married, Sol and Miriam lived with Sol's parents. Sol managed a movie theater. Miriam ran the concession stand. The scenario would be charming except for the fact that they went broke.[1]

Miriam was Jewish because she thought the world of her son, indulged him and protected him, and never, as far as the available evidence suggests, gave him reason to doubt the intensity of her love or the exclusivity of their bond, traits by no means exclusive to Jewish mothers. Yet Doris, his sister, described the feelings around the birth of her brother in terms that revolve around Jewishness: "In a Jewish family, you know, a boy is special. Mother doted on him. He could do no wrong."

A friend of Salinger's from high school wrote, "He was very close to his mother. I met her briefly at the academy and remember her as an attractive and gracious woman, who obviously adored her only son."

It wasn't until after his Bar Mitzvah that Salinger's parents informed their two children that their mother wasn't Jewish. Doris described the experience as "traumatic," and noted that her parents "handled it terribly."

I realize that joking about Solomon's playing down his Jewishness, and also eliding the ham side of his importing business, is glib. I am not going to second-guess anyone's negotiations in the matter of assimilation, especially in an era in which Jews regularly changed their names and had to deal with the real effects of discrimination in a way that is difficult for many American Jews today to comprehend. Yet I have been around enough Jewish businessman fathers on the Upper East Side who have

---

1 Their daughter, Doris, would remark that among their peer group in Chicago, Sol was the only one who didn't make it; this was said with just a little bitterness because though Sol did end up doing very well in his next business, it took a while. J.D. Salinger spent most of his life in relative comfort, and eventually in affluence; Doris, six years older, was much more aware of the transition. "Sonny grew up with money," she remarked to her niece years later.

no clue about literature or culture, a fact for which they feel no remorse, and who have equally little clue about how to talk to their sons, that the picture I have of Sol antagonizes me. It certainly antagonized Salinger, who never said anything nice about his father, and whose body of work is remarkable for being centered on family but with a denuded paternal presence — the father a smudge on an otherwise vivid picture.

Yet Solomon was not passive or benign. He was a self-made man who provided for his family throughout the Depression and beyond. Hamilton, the first Salinger biographer on the scene, communicated with the tight-knit fraternity of cheese importers who still had offices in Tribeca and had known Sol Salinger. Mostly they were second generation; Sol was a peer of their fathers. Solomon was known and admired in business circles for "running a tight ship," Hamilton wrote. "In his later years he was notable for sporting a white mane and a magnificent white beard." As one of the cheese guys put it, "He looked like God."

About Sol's relationship with his son, one of his colleagues said, "I never saw them together."

The Salingers celebrated Christmas and Hanukah, but Solomon identified as Jewish. In 1936 the Federation for the Support of Jewish Philanthropic Societies organized a fund drive around 115 leaders of industry. The *New York Times* listed them all, using extra-small type, with the name of the industry first and then the name of the chairman overseeing fund-raising in that industry. It reads like a prose poem of New York's rising Jewish meritocracy and also an elegy for its era of industrial might. The *B*s alone are an opera: "Bakers and Flour Merchants," "Bankers and Brokers," "Belts, Suspenders, and Garters," "Blouses," "Book Publishers," "Buttons, Mens," "Buttons, Womens." And beside each one, a name. "Dairy Products — Sol Salinger" floats by like a face in the background of a news segment, and, in a similar mode of recognition, I jump at the sight of it, proud that he has made it among all the big Jewish names of the era.

Doris reports that when Sol's mother died, he went to temple every day for a year.

Sol and Miriam's first child, Doris, was born in 1913. Their second child, Jerome, was born on New Year's Day 1919. The birth certificate, Register Number 564, is written in cursive and reflects a certain indecision about the name:

Name of child: "Baby Salinger"
Sex: Male
Color: White
Place of birth: New York Nursery and Child's Hospital. 161 West
    61st St NY
Father's Name: Sol Salinger
Father's Residence: 3681 Broadway
Father's Age: 31
Color: White
Father's Occupation: Cheese Business

After a few days they decided on Jerome David, but began calling him Sonny.

5

The Myron Arms

J.D. SALINGER'S FIRST residence was at 3681 Broadway, an elegant building named the Halidon, situated across from Trinity Church Cemetery in Harlem. From there the family moved several times, always to a better neighborhood, always on Manhattan's Upper West Side. The running-away-from-home-as-an-Indian-with-a-suitcase-full-of-toy-soldiers event took place at 511 West 113th Street between Broadway and Amsterdam in a broad, handsome building in the shadow of Columbia University's Butler Library.

In the late 1920s, the family moved to a spacious apartment at 221 West Eighty-Second Street (now 226 West Eighty-Second) on the corner of Broadway called the Myron Arms. It was designed by Emery Roth, who also created the Beresford and the Eldorado. Though not nearly as grand as those buildings, it attests to Miriam and Sol having a pretty good eye for attractive details, one they passed down to both their children. One can get a sense of the neighborhood's Jewish flavor from the fact that Zabar's, the Jewish delicatessen and cultural institution, opened across the street at Broadway and Eightieth Street in the mid-1930s. It was an up-and-coming neighborhood. Babe Ruth lived just a few blocks away on Riverside Drive.

Salinger attended public school throughout his years on the West Side, though it is clear that Solomon's rising fortunes were changing the way the Salinger family lived. "We had some money by the time Sonny was born," Doris would recall. "That made a big difference."

I found the galley of the Ian Hamilton book. It was in the study of my mother's apartment, located four blocks away from the Myron Arms. My mother's study is a place where you can lose things. There are piles of papers everywhere, sculptures, photographs, and many books, a constellation of random objects from which different stars brightly emerge depending on mood, time of day, and fate. The galley suddenly became visible and was thereafter impossible to miss, perched in plain view atop a uniform row of books whose color was a bluish gray. That yellow cover was so conspicuous. Finding it was like finding a hidden pattern in a drawing, the kind that, as soon as you see it, you can't imagine ever not having been able to make out.

Perhaps I hadn't seen it because my eyes had passed without stopping over that spot with the old books for most of my life. After my tearful reunion with the Hamilton book, I peered at the ancient-looking blue-gray books — an edition of Dickens's novels, including *David Copperfield,* which Holden Caulfield refers to in the first sentence of *The Catcher in the Rye.*

A few years earlier a friend of mine who had spent very little time in New York visited me in this apartment, and the first thing he said after he had taken a seat in the living room and looked around was, "I've never been in one of these kinds of apartments before. It's just like in a J.D. Salinger story!"

"No, no!" I said. "Salinger's stories all take place on the East Side!"

Now I saw that he was onto something. Part of it was the prewar building atmosphere, the feeling of being within a stolid, enormous, labyrinthine ship. But surely he was also responding to the nestlike feeling of an apartment in which lives have grown up and around—which is my romanticized way of describing what could be called clutter (also a feature in Salinger's Glass stories) and, I would like to think, a sense of warmth—the sort of place where you could lose a book.

I had since come to realize my protestation over the neighborhood was not justified. Holden lives on the East Side, and the vast majority of locations in Salinger's stories are set there, including *Franny and Zooey,* but Seymour's prelapsarian youth is set on the West Side, specifically 108th Street and Riverside Drive.

All of Salinger's fiction is city writing, even when it doesn't take place in the city, just as Salinger himself was a city boy for his whole life, even if he spent the majority of his adult life in a rural setting, on a steep hill with a view of mountains. *The Catcher in the Rye* is a city book, a New York book, even if Holden Caulfield doesn't set foot in it until more than a quarter of the way through. New York City is where he has been going that whole time; it is the orienting point of the compass. Seeing the apartment that Salinger grew up in, I decide, is going to be essential to understanding the man, even though I feel as if I have seen it many times in his books. Even though I grew up in a place very much like it myself.

6

Comanches

I N 1930, at age eleven, Sonny was sent to summer camp in
Maine. Camp Wigwam had been founded in 1922 by Abra-
ham Mandelstam, whom everyone called Mandy, and Ar-
nold Lehman, whom everyone called Pop. Mandelstam and
Lehman sounds like a brokerage; Mandy and Pop sounds like
two guys running a camp set directly on the banks of a beautiful lake in western Maine. Both lived in Manhattan most of the
year, except for when camp was in session. This wasn't a hobby;
it was their business, and they co-owned the camp for more
than forty years, running it every summer.

Mandy was probably gay—"An unspoken truth," as Bob
Strauss, the camp's current director, put it. Pop had a wife
named Masie, "a pleasant semibovine person whose loping walk
was often imitated," as Edward Rosen, who first attended Wigwam in 1937, described her.

She was a bit of a recluse and had a hunched back that became a source of fascination at the camp. At one point it
emerged that campers had developed an unauthorized tradition
of traipsing into the woods to urinate on a strangely shaped tree
that, they felt, mimicked the shape of Masie's hunched back.
Enraged, Pop had the tree cut down. It was dragged back behind the rifle range. It was duly discovered, with the result that
everyone now snuck off to urinate on the tree behind the rifle
range. Apparently the campers were insatiable in their desire to

urinate on Masie's likeness. Either out of good humor or a desire to keep kids from hanging out behind the rifle range, Pop had the tree dragged back to its original spot and resurrected it with boards and nails. A plaque was added. It became a statue of its former self. The tree is now gone but the plaque, which reads MASIE'S TREE, remains.

In 1934, four years after Salinger attended Camp Wigwam, Mandy and Pop had a fight and stopped talking to each other. For the next thirty years, during which they ran the camp together, supervised throngs of screaming kids at play, oversaw meals, hired counselors, hustled parents to enroll their kids over the winter and greeted these same parents with open arms on parents' day in the middle of summer, they spoke "only when necessary and never with any cordiality that I saw," said Rosen.

In the early 1960s Pop sold out his share to Mandy, and a couple of years later, in 1964, Mandy sold to Ned and Helen Strauss. Ned threw out his back in 1976, and his son, Bob, who grew up on the property, took over that same year. He has run the camp ever since and lives there year-round with his family.

I showed up in early March to have a look around. There had been a huge storm the day before, but on the day of my visit the sky was utterly clear and the air was soft. I had raced up from Boston, making such good time on the interstate that I was lulled into a false confidence. I dallied in a few spots, once to have lunch and then in a sudden panic about the need for galoshes.

I had never before set foot in Maine. When I crossed the border I noted the braggadocio of the welcome sign — LIFE AS IT SHOULD BE — immediately followed by a sign promising dire consequences for drunk drivers. I had not been able to find galoshes. The sun was going down, a rapid descent. I turned onto progressively smaller roads. The moisture in the air made the light diffuse and lovely. The landscape was beautiful but I couldn't enjoy it, as I was too worried that it would be dark when I arrived and also that my one pair of shoes would be covered in frozen mud. I finally pulled over and bought some garbage bags with the idea that I would wrap my feet in them.

Summer camps in winter are a bit like college campuses at the start of summer — both are totally out of character and yet are, somehow, especially evocative of themselves. Something about the absent bodies, all the voices you know once filled the place, and will again, but are for now silent.

Bob Strauss emerged from his house, at the edge of an enormous snow-covered lake, just as I was stepping into a black garbage bag.

"I'm worried about mud," I said.

"You're going to be slipping all over the place," he said. "You don't need it."

We first entered the dining hall — wood floors, a vaulted ceiling, a big old stove. Sun came crashing in through the windows overlooking the lake. The lake's canoes had been brought inside and glowed dormant in the sun. I felt for a second that shiver of chilliness a kid might feel upon entering this space in the morning for breakfast. There were pictures from most of the summers up on the walls. We found one from 1922, but we couldn't find one from 1930.

We headed off in the direction of the cabins. "Follow in my footsteps," said Bob. The air came out of my mouth in puffs, and my feet, much bigger than Bob's, had some trouble finding the exact spot where he had stepped. The whole visit was on the verge of turning into a very difficult game of hopscotch. I was so busy trying to place my feet into the holes he had made in the snow I couldn't look around. Halfway through the field I said to hell with it and looked up. We were approaching a group of cabins arranged in a crescent facing the field. The sun had moved behind the trees, but the sky was still a cheerful blue, and the lake, visible through the trees, glowed white.

When we got closer I saw that each cabin had the name of an

Indian tribe on it. I went right for the one that said COMAN-CHES. Not because there was any explicit evidence that Salinger had stayed there. But in "The Laughing Man," the children were Comanches. It felt right. We stepped into the darkness of the cabin. I stood within the cold wooden walls, the sense of enclosure enhanced by the bluish light outside. In summer this place would be clattering with voices. Now, in the silence of winter, snow on the ground at dusk, I heard them loud and clear. My own memories of camp flooded in. For me, camp was a respite from a much more brutal social life that I had at school. I thought, in a semiabstract way, of the positive energy that *The Catcher in the Rye* injected into the eighth-grade canon. Other books from that group had a much darker vision — *A Separate Peace, Animal Farm, 1984,* and that dystopian classic of eighth-grade literature that haunts every gathering of young boys: *Lord of the Flies.*

I looked around. The stillness of the trees, the sense of anticipation in that crescent of cabins around the field, the open space of the lake. I was standing within a lovely circuit where the positive energy of this camp flowed into little Sonny Salinger, who won the award for best actor here in 1930, at age eleven, and for whom the recreational gatherings of youth — on field trips, in day camp, in summer camp — would always have a honeyed glow, which in turn was evoked in writing, which was then imbibed by a boy who would later come sloshing through fields of deep, wet snow on a pilgrimage to the Comanche cabin of Salinger's youth, and his own.

We began to walk through the stand of pines to the shore of the lake. Bob was telling me about the history of Mandy and Pop, the long silence between them like a doughnut hole amid the sweet, overwhelming noise of a summer camp in Maine.

The last thing I did was shuffle out onto the lake for Bob to take a picture of me with my phone. He was telling me that Masie, in her old age, lived nearby all year round, and was cared

for by a local. She would come by now and then, long after Pop
and Mandy were gone, for brief glimpses of the camp.

I took a few steps and tamped my foot on the ice, testing.

"Nothing to worry about," said Bob. He seemed competent,
calm, kind. I thought he must be a good camp director. Later
I would sit with his wife and college-age daughter in his living
room, sipping hot chocolate by the fire, and regard him as almost a peer, another grown-up hustling and trying to enjoy his
life. But now, on the lake's ice, he was one of those remote, almost godlike figures, the grown-ups, a level above the counselors even, one of those people whom you wanted to deceive half
the time and the other half depended on for meals, protection,
and advice on such matters as when to stop walking out onto a
frozen lake.

I shuffled out a few more steps, then a few more. "That's
fine," he said, his voice a little tight.

I turned gingerly to face him, wondering if I had gone too
far. The sun was blasting onto the hills behind the far side of
the lake. Camp Wigwam and most of the lake was in shadow,
settling into a misty dusk. The picture he took shows the lake's
white surface, the rich blue sky above, a brightly lit landscape in
the distance, and a silhouette in the foreground, which seems
an appropriate way to render a biographer moving through the
long-ago landscape of his subject's summer camp.

1932: McBurney and Central Park

I N 1932, at the lowest point of the Depression, Solomon Salinger moved his family across town to 1133 Park Avenue, at Ninety-First Street. Having been in both apartments, I can attest that the new place was bigger, but not that much bigger. Its main distinction was that it was on Park Avenue. Yet it should be noted that 1133 is very modest by the standards of Park Avenue, with a tiny lobby and two reasonably sized apartments on every floor, and that it was north of Eighty-Sixth Street, and would have been a rental at the time they moved in. But it was, then and now, Park Avenue, and surely a moment of pride for Solomon and Miriam Salinger.

For Sonny it was also a moment of uprooting. Not only did he leave the Jewish Upper West Side for the WASPy Upper East Side, he was enrolled in a private school for the first time. Dalton, one of the city's elite private schools, was just blocks away. Salinger was enrolled in McBurney, not so elite and now defunct, which was located back on the West Side, on West Sixty-Third Street, just off Central Park West. In his admissions interview with McBurney, Salinger said he could "swim fifty feet; liked ping pong, soccer and tropical fish." Academics, it turned out, held no interest for him. He lasted two years and then flunked out. But in his two years at McBurney he was an engaged student in other ways. He was class vice president, then class president. He was a reporter on the school paper, the *McBurnian*. He

acted in two school plays, continuing his Camp Wigwam spe-
cialization by playing the female lead in each. A review of one of
those plays in the *McBurnian,* for which Salinger wrote theater
reviews, praised his performance; it is suspiciously unsigned.

There is one detail from his McBurney years that jumps
out — he was friends with a boy named Bobby Strasser who
died suddenly of a sinus infection. Salinger's fiction is so shot
through with the grief of a lost sibling — a brother — and yet he
never lost a sibling and didn't have a brother. Was he shaken by
the death of his close friend Bobby Strasser?

Strasser's mother reported to Hamilton that Salinger and
her son had never been very close, though they were colleagues
on the McBurney student council.

Salinger's failure at McBurney and his being asked to leave
seem, at first, to provide a neat answer to the question of why
Salinger had such animosity toward the world's Ivy League–ish
phonies. It would be natural, if a bit reductive, to think that a
kid who did badly at school would sneer at those who did well.
But the roots of these feelings go in many directions, including
the anti-Semitism then prevalent in the Ivy League milieu.

McBurney makes a notable cameo in *The Catcher in the Rye*
as the school with which Pencey Prep is supposed to have a fenc-
ing meet, except Holden loses the foils on the subway so the
meet never takes place. Salinger's primary association with Mc-
Burney, it seems, was humiliation. But was McBurney its source?

Much of McBurney's significance, for me, lies in its location.
Salinger's writing constantly references the landscape of the city,
and in the city's landscape one can find echoes of his writing.
But can you find echoes of his life? If you stand in Central Park
down near Sixty-Third, just west of the Wollman ice-skating
rink and the big rock outcropping, as I did one freezing winter day, you can see, rising up like some prehistoric beast about
halfway down the block amid the bright limestone of the other
buildings, the old sooty building of the McBurney YMCA. It

would not have been sooty when he went there, but it would have been just as conspicuous. If you pivot east from that same vantage point, you would be on a direct course to the pond and its ducks, about whose winter activities Holden Caulfield famously inquires. In *The Catcher in the Rye,* when Holden asks the cabdriver about the ducks in winter, there is no mention of McBurney. Or of high school. Or of being asked to leave with an accompanying letter that states he had "been hit hard by adolescence," as Salinger had. And yet that question is infused by a winsome loneliness and a sense of solitude that a winter walk that starts at McBurney and enters Central Park must have held. You can feel it there today.

"He wanted to do unconventional things," said a contemporary of Salinger's, who knew him in 1932, at the time of his enrollment in the McBurney School. "For hours, nobody in the family knew where he was or what he was doing. He just showed up for meals."

A lot can happen in the interval between school and home, especially when school and home are two points at opposite corners of Central Park. The park pops up in a number of famous Salinger scenes — the ducks-in-winter scene of *The Catcher in the Rye,* the Saturday day camp in "The Laughing Man" — but its presence, and that of the city in general, asserts itself in all kinds of ways that are less quantifiable. Writers are sometimes asked about their influences, and the truth is that many of them are nonliterary and often unconscious. The streetlamps in Central Park at dusk, or the gray hexagonal-block sidewalks that line the perimeter of the park, which look the same today as they did when J.D. Salinger was a kid, are present in his writing without ever being mentioned. The city is itself a worn and used thing, the stones smoothed by a million heels pounding on them like tidal waves on rocks, its landscape unforgiving but also a refuge to which one can adapt, and within which one can, at least for an afternoon, disappear.

The Salinger Triptych

A FTER A PERIOD of contemplating Salinger's work, I find that it begins to arrange itself in triptych form.

Left panel: his early work. Starting in 1940 with his first published story, and extending into 1948. The stories from this period are generally looked at as apprentice work; many critics brush them aside. This is a mistake. There are several gems ("A Girl I Knew," "The Stranger," "The Last and Best of the Peter Pans," "A Young Girl in 1941 with No Waist at All," "A Boy in France"), as well as stories that are precursors to other stories that are gems—the man hardly ever wrote a story without slightly reiterating a story he had written before. Holden Caulfield appears in one of his earliest stories, "Slight Rebellion off Madison." Written in 1941, it is the first story that he sold to *The New Yorker*. It would have been his fourth published story, but Pearl Harbor was attacked a week before it was scheduled to run at the end of 1941, at which point the magazine decided it was no longer appropriate to the tenor of the times.

Center panel: The panel is inaugurated with "A Perfect Day for Bananafish," published in the January 31, 1948, issue of *The New Yorker*. A contemporary of Salinger's, Roger Angell, who was working at the magazine at the time, described the appearance of that story as being "like a shot. No one had ever read anything like that before." Salinger's work in this panel runs through 1957, but since he waited so long to collect these stories into book form, it has its final closure with the publication of his last book, *Raise High the Roof Beam, Carpenters and Seymour: An Introduction,* in 1963.

Right panel: Contains one published piece of writing, "Hapworth 16, 1924," published in *The New Yorker* in 1965. Otherwise it is barren of writing by Salinger, though it features a lot of writing *about* Salinger. It spans half his lifetime, from 1963 to 2010.

The Salinger triptych is a strange thing to contemplate. Of course it is a natural impulse to take an author's work and break it into sections or periods. For example, Philip Roth. *Goodbye, Columbus* and the next two novels, *Letting Go* and *When She Was Good,* would be the first panel, defined by a conservative style, however ebullient. The center panel would begin with the radical break of *Portnoy's Complaint* and stretch through the alter ego books of Zuckerman and Kepesh, the formal experiments becoming more and more pronounced and culminating in *The Counterlife* and *Operation Shylock.*

At this point the third panel begins, with another explosive departure, *Sabbath's Theater.* Except now he has come full circle, and there are no more formal games, and he is back, in some sense, in New Jersey. But instead of peering at his girlfriend's father as some primitive, a Jew who is so worshipful of money that the plumbing gasket on which the family fortune rests sits in a glass vitrine in their home, he now takes up the point of view of that generation, or his generation at that age, with much more sympathy. And then *American Pastoral,* at which point the Newark chronicles begin, and in some sense Roth is working the same territory evoked by the list of Jewish Federation industry chairmen that Sol Salinger appeared on in 1936, published in the *New York Times,* all the Jewish *machers* of New York listed next to the industry they represented.

Roth's third panel is a hugely productive push, through *The Human Stain* and on to *Nemesis.* All the way to the very public retirement, so formal I wonder if there wasn't cake and a gold watch. It's almost as if he's managed to normalize the whole crazy enterprise of being Philip Roth and be a glove manufacturer who has decided to move to Florida — followed by the equivalent of postcards from Roth, with phrases like "This not writing thing is great!" scrawled on the back, written from a pool somewhere as he floats on a raft with a colorful drink in his hand.

What stands out about the Roth triptych — and it doesn't have to be a triptych of course, it could be more panels or fewer — is that the panels are composed of books available to any reader.

But that is not the case with the Salinger triptych. All of the work he is known for is in the center panel. *The Catcher in the Rye, Nine Stories, Franny and Zooey, Raise High the Roof Beam, Carpenters and Seymour: An Introduction.* All the famous work is on that middle panel, but not all the fame. And not all the work. There are a book's worth of good stories on the first panel, a number of them fantastic works, and there is the mystery library of the third panel. One could say about the Salinger triptych: He was a writer. Then a famous author. Then a myth.

J.D. Salinger was a ferociously productive, dedicated writer who enjoyed enormous success at a young age. He published in the highest-paying and most widely read magazines of the day. When, as a soldier stationed in Europe during World War II, he sought out Ernest Hemingway, the famous author received him, not as a peer, certainly, but as a particularly fresh-faced colleague. Hemingway knew who he was, having read Salinger's story "This Sandwich Has No Mayonnaise" in *Esquire.* They ran a picture of Salinger alongside the story, so Hemingway might have recognized the face. Young writers are often asked to have their faces appear alongside their work.

The Salinger of the center panel was sufficiently aggrieved

by the presence of his photograph on the back of *Catcher* that by the time it went into its third edition he had successfully petitioned for its removal. The Salinger of the third panel would agree to have only one thing published at all. But the first-panel Salinger was happy enough to be in *Esquire,* which was a notch above the other slicks that were buying his stories in terms of prestige.

Salinger intended to collect these early stories in a book, and only a trick of fate prevented it from happening. And then he later decided to suppress the stories. He didn't want them read. They are a chimera, a rumor, but also in plain sight.

9

1934–1936: Salinger the Sublime

SCHOOLS THAT EXPEL KIDS usually feel the need to be clear about their reasons, which they articulate in a letter. McBurney expelled Salinger and in an accompanying letter described him as "fuzzy." It said he had "plenty" of ability. Regarding industry: "He did not know the word."

It was not easy to find a school that would take J.D. Salinger. Eventually, in the fall of 1934, he was accepted at Valley Forge Military Academy, a relatively new boarding school located in rural Pennsylvania, half an hour outside of Philadelphia.

There are some conspicuous similarities with *The Catcher in the Rye*'s Pencey Prep: Both ran advertisements in the *New York Times* featuring a guy on a horse, but had no horses. Both presented themselves as a kind of shaper-upper of misfits. Valley Forge's *Times* ad used the phrase "Educational Troubleshooters." Also, in the novel and in real life, the dorm rooms were separated by shared showers, and privacy in the rooms was minimal. But the similarities are mostly cosmetic.

Salinger's sister, Doris, thought it was an anti-Semitic environment and that Salinger suffered for being a Jew. A survey taken at the time that showed this area of central Pennsylvania to have some of the most anti-Semitic attitudes in the country might back her up, but if this was part of his experience Salinger rarely wrote or said anything about it, with the exception of "Down at the Dinghy," in which the four-year-old protagonist is nursing a moral grievance it takes the whole story to tease out — the housekeeper called his father a "big sloppy kike." Salinger would later claim to have been writing stories since the age of fifteen, when he was in his first year at Valley Forge. He wrote at night, under the covers with a flashlight. McBurney, affiliated with the YMCA, was the setting for his discovery that he wasn't Jewish. Perhaps Valley Forge was the setting for reminding him that he was.

At Valley Forge Salinger was sarcastic and aloof, but he was also funny, engaged, involved. He made friends. And, though it's not explicit, he experienced for the first time the strange prerogative and temptation of the New Yorker exiled to the provinces: the opportunity to be Mr. New York.

Hamilton elicited several testimonials from his classmates:

"What I remember most about Jerome was the way he used to speak. He always talked in a pretentious manner as if he were reciting something from Shakespeare."

"I must say I enjoyed his company immensely. He was full of wit and humor and sizzling wisecracks. He was a precocious and gifted individual, and I think he realized at that age that he was more gifted with the pen than the rest of us."

"We were both skinny adolescents and must have looked terribly young and boyish. I was immensely attracted to him because of his sophistication and humor. His conversation was frequently laced with sarcasm about others and the silly routines we had to obey and follow at school. Both of us hated the military regime and often wondered why we didn't leave the school. I believe Jerry did everything he could not to earn a cadet promotion, which he considered childish and absurd. He enjoyed breaking the rules, and several times we both slipped off the academy grounds at 4 am to enjoy breakfast in the local diner. It was a great surprise to me that he returned to school the second year."

"He loved conversation. He was given to mimicry. He liked people, but he couldn't stand stuffed shirts. Jerry was aware that he was miscast in the military role. He was all legs and angles, very slender, with a shock of black hair combed backwards. His uniform was always rumpled in the wrong places. He always stuck out like a sore thumb in a long line of cadets."

One day Salinger's mother came to visit and commented on the "red flashes" that some boys had on their hats. Salinger told her this indicated that the boys had been punished for using profane language and were to be avoided. In fact, they were badges of merit.

He snuck off campus, got drunk sometimes, was aloof and sardonic, but he managed to avoid serious trouble. Only once did things veer into the realm of a major setback: One night he got extremely drunk and started making a lot of noise, talking about breaking out of the school, and generally raising enough hell that it was going to be acknowledged by the authorities. This auto-da-fé was extinguished by a knockout punch delivered by his roommate, Ned Davis — a possible model for Stradlater in *The Catcher in the Rye*. Of Davis, one of his classmates reports: "Ned was a fine cadet, but he was good looking, tall, combed his hair constantly and believed himself to be the answer to a woman's prayer."

There was another, more positive side to Salinger's Valley Forge experience. He was a committed booster and enthusiast of the school, a joiner. He belonged to the glee club, the aviation club, the French club, and the drama club, called Mask and Spur. He played the male lead in a World War I melodrama in which one of his lines was: "Oh, but good Lord, that must have been simply topping." (Another: "The Germans are really quite decent, aren't they?")

Among his classmates Salinger was already "the writer."

"Jerry was never much in a hurry as far as moving was concerned," said one. "He was a very advanced thinker. I mean, he always came up with a different angle on things. When we wanted to spell a word, we'd hit him."

Salinger was the literary editor of the class yearbook, *Crossed Sabres,* which is to say he wrote it. It is filled with seemingly straight-faced cheers and homages, such as this one to the school's founder, headmaster, and majordomo, Colonel Baker: "When one thinks of Valley Forge Military Academy one thinks of Colonel Baker. The names are synonymous. All that Valley Forge has meant to us, Colonel Baker has meant to us. We, the Class of 1936, here regretfully take leave of this man, who has embodied all we ever hope to be."

It is true that once you know that the author of the above would insult someone by saying, "John, you're a prince of a guy," it's tempting to wonder if these words are facetious. Hamilton suspects as much. But I think Salinger was being sincere. You simply cannot overstate the sense of gratitude and reprieve a kid will feel toward the school that rescues him from the cesspool of the old school that has thrown him out.

In the spring 1935 edition of *Crossed Sabres,* his first year there, he is given the nickname "Salinger the Sublime."

The 1936 edition, his senior year, includes Salinger's musing on his class's pending graduation: "September, 1932, the beginning of a new life! Prep School! Do you remember with what anxiety you waited for the order to report and, after it arrived, the feeling of trepidation on suddenly being faced with the realization that the die was really cast; that you were actually leaving your parents and friends — your accustomed habits — for a military school, about which you had read so much and looked forward to with such longing? Do you remember the sharp emotion of bidding mother goodbye and the firm handclasp of father before you were hustled away by the important looking cadets at the Plebe detail?"

This is fiction. Salinger arrived not in 1932 but in 1934.

On one hand this smudging of facts can be dismissed as an attempt to manufacture a shared history. But it also sounds like the equivalent of one of those doctored Soviet photographs in which some disgraced party official is airbrushed out of history save for his hat, which he had lent to the dear leader who remains in the photograph.[1] McBurney has disappeared.

A lie is a form of wishing, but what was Salinger wishing for? Perhaps he wanted simply to write McBurney out of his personal history, the way people expunge certain difficult romances from their personal history. But if we take him seriously, perhaps it really was 1932, the year his family moved from the Myron Arms on West Eighty-Second Street to 1133 Park Avenue, that was the occasion for "bidding goodbye" to his mother, and the dawn of the remote handclasp of his father — perhaps it was around the time when he found out he wasn't Jewish, or not in the way he thought, that his parents came to feel like strangers.

Salinger composed a song for the class of 1936 that was published in *Crossed Sabres* and sung at graduation. It begins:

> *Hide not thy tears on this last day*
> *Your sorrow has no shame*
> *To march no more midst lines of gray,*
> *no longer play the game.*

It goes on at length in this vein. Incredibly, it is sung to this day at the school's graduation ceremonies.

Ian Hamilton thinks all this is a straight-faced performance that masks a more sneering irony in keeping with Salinger's gen-

---

1 An image drawn from the Milan Kundera novel *The Book of Laughter and Forgetting.*

eral disposition. "The 'terrific liar' is at his most effective when he starts believing his own lies," he writes. Perhaps.

But saving and being saved figure largely in Salinger's imagination, as we know from *The Catcher in the Rye,* and Valley Forge saved him in several ways. No matter how foolish he thought its rituals, the school was there for him when he was in need. Holden Caulfield famously flees a prep school for which he has disdain and at which he was a mess. But that is a transposition of Salinger's feeling toward McBurney onto the slightly pompous institution of Valley Forge.

10

The Perversities of Princeton

I HEAD TO PRINCETON University's library, where there are copies of Salinger's early stories and his correspondence with his first editor and writing instructor, Whit Burnett.

On the train down from Penn Station I am excited to be taking on the role of literary sleuth, though I am aware that there is a long and undistinguished history of people getting excited about investigating Salinger — they always sound like self-aggrandizing burglars. Or, as Salinger himself put it in his letter to Hamilton,[1] writing in the baroque, practically Jamesian ornateness of his late style: "I might just add, probably not at all wisely, that it has always been a terrible and almost inassimilable wonder to me that it is evidently quite lawful, the world over, for a newspaper or publishing house to 'commission' somebody, in the not particular fair name of good journalism or basic profitable academic research..."

It's an awful experience to read the second, published, Hamilton biography after you have read the first, suppressed, one. The second book lacks Salinger's voice, but its shortcomings go far beyond this omission. Hamilton's attempt to take a terse, straightforward, and highly literate act of biography and turn it into an extended personal essay fails, in part because the air of joviality feels forced amid the acrid smell of legal bitterness

---

1 Later quoted in *New York* magazine's June 15, 1987, cover story on the case.

hanging over it all. Hamilton does not say in the first book, as he does in the second, that Salinger "was, in any real-life sense, invisible, as good as dead."

Wilfrid Sheed, reviewing *In Search of J.D. Salinger* in the *New York Review of Books,* would quip in response that there is "a small but crucial distinction between dead and invisible."

The aura of trespass is strong around Salinger. It hovers over the rituals of the Princeton archives. Salinger's papers, and Hamilton's, are located in the Dulles Reading Room. I must leave nearly everything but my computer in a locker and wash my hands. Cleansed and disarmed, I enter the chapel with its vaulted ceiling. It is a marvelously hushed room, an octagonal shape. Eight tables face the librarian's desk at the head of the room. At the back of the room is a computer terminal. At the sides of the room are large metal cabinets for boxes from the archives that have been ordered in advance. At a certain point in the day someone hits a switch and the gauzy white blinds that have been deflecting the morning sun are lifted to the sky, resulting, as far as I could tell, in no change whatsoever in the light or in the view. But it is another sacrament in the holy place, nonetheless.

The first thing I do is spend time looking at the box with Ian Hamilton's working papers for his Salinger biography. That Princeton is where these are kept seems slightly perverse. Princeton is also home to the story archive, filled with Salinger's letters, quite a few of which Hamilton quoted in his book that he was then not allowed to publish. I had brought my galley of this suppressed Hamilton book. It lay on the table next to his box of papers. The room now held Salinger's private, unpublished musings in three separate versions.

While I peer at Hamilton's fastidious handwriting, a box from the story archives containing Salinger's letters and early stories is brought to a separate table.

With the Hamilton material I can sit with my laptop and type notes as I read. The Salinger material has a special rule.

The rule is that you may not have anything with you at your table when you sit with the Salinger box. No computer. No pencil. Just you and the letters.

I don't rush over. I wait a bit. The box sits there like an urn. I peer at it: a box full of the very Salinger letters on which Hamilton had once taken notes while sitting in this room. Notes that I am now reading, and that he put in his book that sits by my side, after which one could no longer take notes on the Salinger material, which is why it is now sitting on a separate table.

I move to the Salinger table. My laptop is one table behind me. Whenever I read something I wish to quote I stand up from the Salinger table and walk over to the table with my laptop. At first I did this in a solemn spirit, moving slowly, because this was not a room for haste. But gradually I began to speed up. You can hold on to only so much at a time. Salinger's letters had some wonderful bits, and I wanted to write them down. The librarian said nothing about my moving from one table to another. It was a formality whose purpose completely escaped me. Eventually I found myself dashing between the two tables as though I were carrying handfuls of water to fill a tub.

If the atmosphere surrounding the laws and ethics of intellectual property and copyright wasn't strong enough just from the procedures attached to these letters, there was another layer that I could sense but didn't understand until later. It had to do with the wonderful notepaper provided by the reading room — because you could not bring in any paper of your own. It was lined, Princeton orange, and had a hole in the center.

I later discovered that Princeton, among all the great old universities, was the last to discard its library's honor system for a more conventional approach. It did this sometime in the 1970s, shutting down the whole library to take an inventory, upon which librarians discovered that all sorts of priceless manuscripts and documents were missing. Stolen. Princeton had been robbed blind for decades.

The conflicts of intellectual property surround the whole university and the town.

"Princeton probably regrets calling itself Princeton," said a colleague of mine who had gone there, Roger Bellin.

"Why is that?" I asked.

"Because they can't trademark the name. It's the name of a town. Anyone can use it. Harvard and Yale and Dartmouth all get to charge huge licensing fees if someone wants to use their name. The Princeton Review, for example, has nothing to do with the university."

Finally there is the role of Princeton itself in Salinger's work. The very train platform I step out onto that freezing bright morning is the platform where Lane Coutell famously stands, with his coat open, reading a letter from the girl who will soon be disembarking at the station, Franny.

But this has to be pointed out to me by a former student, Nick Peruffo, whom I meet for lunch; he has gotten a job in nearby Trenton as a sportswriter. When I tell him what brought me here, he references "Franny" and the misunderstanding about the location.

"I thought the scene at the station took place in New Haven," I tell him.

"A lot of people do," he said. "I got this lecture on iTunes U about Salinger, and the professor makes the same mistake. She talks about how it's in New Haven. But that's because they talk about 'the Yale Game.' But no one at Yale would refer to a home game as the Yale Game. You would only say that if you were in a school where Yale was the away team. Like Princeton."

Further investigation revealed the restaurant where Lane and Franny dined was called Sickler's, which was modeled after Lahiere's, which, though now closed, was still in business on Princeton's Witherspoon Street as recently as 2010. Frogs' legs were on the menu.

11

Samizdat Salinger

THE DULLES READING ROOM closes at 4:45 p.m. I head back to the train station. It's already dark, and bitterly cold in a way that seems appropriate to my subject. Salinger weather is one that favors coats, scarves, sweaters. I make my way back down past unfamiliar buildings, hoping to bump into the train station. It is winter break and the campus is deserted. A campus shuttle picks me up, and the driver makes a special stop for me, his only passenger. He tells me it's a shortcut, and instructs me to go up the hill. I find myself behind some building in the dark, scrambling upward amid damp leaves and shrubbery. Eventually I see the station but it is on the other side of a fence, which I have to walk along for a while. I feel like a burglar.

On my last visit to the Princeton library before heading down to New Orleans, I get set up with my laptop in the Dulles Reading Room, summon one of the boxes from the story archives, and watch as it is placed on a table in front of the one where I sit. I let it sit there on the other table. By the end of the day I stand to leave without having so much as touched the box. I open the lid for a moment on my way out, as though to let some emanation into the air. Then I close it, and set off into the brightly lucid late afternoon.

In New York I go straight from the train to a restaurant where I will collect one more piece of contraband Salinger. The man I am meeting is an acquaintance, a movie guy. Used to be a music guy. One of these characters who makes things seem effortless; success surrounds him like weather. When I had mentioned my biography he said that he was a Salinger freak and in possession of the samizdat edition of Salinger's short stories, the publications of the first panel of the Salinger triptych.

In the early 1970s someone had collected these stories into a pair of slender pamphlets. The typeface was small, the font was that of a computer printer, and he or she had clearly typed in some haste, because there are typos. An amateurish job that nevertheless managed to sell about twenty-five thousand copies at bookstores around the country before Salinger got wind of it and sued to have it stopped. It was these circumstances that occasioned his granting a rare interview. He told Lacey Fosburgh[1]

---

1 Fosburgh had been an assistant to then *New York Times* culture editor Arthur Gelb, who recalls her energy and her confidence. Specifically, she had often remarked that one day she would get an interview with J.D. Salinger. Gelb would ask how she planned to get it. She said she didn't know. Her husband, the author David Harris, recounted the circumstances by which it happened:

> By virtue of her incredible charisma as a reporter Lacey made it easy to talk, and knew how to get people to talk. She was totally surprised at the phone call. She had put in the obligatory call to Salinger's representative when the story broke, assumed she would write a story saying he declined comment. And then the phone rings. I picked it up, listened for a moment, and called out, "There is a man named Salinger who wants to talk to you." I gave her the phone, and all of a sudden she's saying, "Get me something to write with!" And she just kept him on the phone. I could see her keeping the thing going. I don't imagine there was any dead space in that conversation. Every time he stopped talking she came up with another question. When the phone went down, she celebrated. She was very full of her triumph, happy. "That was J.D. Salinger!"

Fosburgh died of cancer in 1993. Harris was describing his late wife, mother of his kids, who died twenty years ago, as she was twenty years before that. His of the *New York Times* in 1974: "Some stories, my property, have been stolen," Salinger said about the unauthorized publication. "Someone's appropriated them. It's an illicit act. It's unfair. Suppose you had a coat you liked and somebody went into your closet and stole it. That's how I feel."

The paradox of this quintessentially Salingerian metaphor is that in order to appreciate it fully one has to have read one of his uncollected stories, "This Sandwich Has No Mayonnaise," which contains the following lines: "Who swiped my raincoat? With all my letters in the left-hand pocket. My letters from Red, from Phoebe, from Holden. From Holden. Aw, listen, I don't care about the raincoat being swiped, but how about leaving my letters alone?"

At the bar, I slide the two dun-colored pamphlets, staple bound, into my bag, but not before promising my friend to take good care of them and noting the price he paid, written on the inside in faint antiquarian pencil markings: $600. I have a new bag that my wife gave me for the holidays. A leather satchel. The samizdat Salinger sits snugly beside the samizdat Ian Hamilton biography, which itself contains more samizdat Salinger. I am a walking repository of illicit Salinger.

Because of my misadventure with the Hamilton galley I vow to keep all these books in the leather bag at all times. Which is not to say I read the pamphlets. Some people splurge and some people savor. These stories are a finite resource, after all. How

---

voice was clear, serene, but very focused, as though he were summoning a holograph for us both.

In those days you called stories in. So later that night, she called in and read the piece. The *Times* ran it on the front page. In those days a piece of soft news running on the front page didn't happen very often. She got a lot of professional recognition out of it. I am glad for her to get that recognition . . . a wonderful person, an extraordinary person.

many times will one be able to read a new Salinger story? There are two ways to respond to a secret when one comes into your possession: You share it with everyone, or you keep it, and delight in being part of a conspiracy of virtue. In this book I want to do both.

1937: Vienna

AFTER JERRY SALINGER graduated from Valley Forge in 1936 he returned to 1133 Park Avenue. That fall he enrolled at New York University. Living at home and taking a bus to school had not gone well when he attended McBurney. The results at NYU were no better. When his midterm grades arrived in the spring of 1937 he dropped out.

Salinger was not without direction at this point. He had aspirations. He was going to be a writer. Maybe an actor. Also a playwright. He was going to write short stories, or he was going to write plays, or both; it was not entirely clear. None of it appealed to Solomon Salinger. He decided that the next step would be for his academically ungifted son to learn the import business via an extended apprenticeship in Europe. Salinger's first stop would be a five-month stay in Vienna, where he would polish his language skills, and then a shorter stay in Poland, where he would get acquainted with what went into the tins of picnic hams that J.S. Hoffman and Co. so profitably imported.

Examining these fraught years in the run-up to World War II and trying to project backward through time to what everyone was thinking, or should have been thinking, is nearly impossible. The events loom too large. Then there is the peril of the righteousness in hindsight. Nevertheless I cannot help but wonder if Sol's unconscious hostility toward Sonny was so strong that he would send his Jewish son to Vienna in 1937.

But, incredibly, it turns out that during the summer of 1937 Vienna was seen as a tourist hot spot. In August of that year the *New York Times* lauded the city's virtues for travelers: "The lull in Austrian politics has played its part in attracting tourists. Consequently, the populace itself is seeing to it that no Nazi demonstrations occur. In some towns turbulent Nazi youths have been promptly squelched by the citizenry"—thereby suggesting a previously unexplored rationale for German resistance to Hitler as he consolidated power: He'll kill the tourist trade!

I go back and forth with this slightly ridiculous bit of travel advice. On one hand it makes Vienna seem like a plausible place for Solomon to send his son so that he might learn the language and the ham and cheese import trade; on the other hand I keep picturing a fifteen-year-old Jewish boy who lived there in the shadow of the Prater, the city's famous amusement park, with its gigantic Ferris wheel — my father.

Seen from this angle, the fact that there are turbulent Nazi youth in need of squelching is terrifying. Reading that line I feel a bit like the narrator of Delmore Schwartz's classic story "In Dreams Begin Responsibilities," who watches his parents' courtship unfold on the screen and shouts, "Don't do it!" In my version I see a very young man moving through the city where he was born and raised, perhaps walking with his older brother along the Ringstrasse in the evening to see the opera, and I want to yell, Get out now!

My father's childhood in Vienna has always been mysterious to me.

My father and his immediate family did get out, more or less at the final possible moment. The last to leave the city was the youngest, my father. But my father died when I was just turning ten, and I heard all this not directly from him, but from my mother, who tends to inflect stories with a fairy-tale aura. Yet I take at face value the central image of his escape: My father running from a train station through a dark forest in the middle of the night until he falls into "the frozen water"[1] and swims, or simply floats, across, where he is pulled out by Swiss soldiers and put in the best kind of camp a Viennese Jew in the aftermath of the Anschluss could end up in — the kind preceded by the word "refugee."

What is so strange about contemplating Salinger embarking on a cruise ship across the ocean at this time is that it makes me realize how I have been practicing the biographical gaze — more like a squint — in which one pieces together available facts with bits of speculation and circumstance, for much of my life — it feels as if I have been trailing a suspect through crowded streets and into a strange room, where all of a sudden I see someone I know. I want to wave, across the distance of seventy-five years, at them both.

Pondering this intersection of Salinger and my father, I can't decide which seems more unlikely: that the Bar Mitzvahed, college-age son of a Jewish ham and cheese magnate from Manhattan should end up living with a Jewish family in Vienna in 1937, or that a fifteen-year-old, not-well-off Jewish boy living in the shadow of the Prater and its famous Ferris wheel would, within a few years, be living on New York City's teeming Lower East

---

1 Salinger's generation has now been beatified as the "Greatest Generation," but at the time it was known as the "Silent Generation." This was even truer of the refugees from Europe, who were so reluctant to discuss the details of their experiences that each family would, over generations, engage in a form of linguistic scrapbooking in which a few uttered phrases would take on the status of artifacts. "The frozen water" is such a phrase in my family. But it stands alone, and all the adornments I have been able to summon to provide context feel like conservators' additions, not the real thing. Thus, pressing my mother on the matter of whether he "fell" or "jumped" into the water, she reports that he said he fell. "He didn't see it?" I ask. "It was very dark," she says. "But if he was intending to swim across, why did he fall?" I ask. "He was in a hurry, and it may have started sooner than he thought," she says. But we both know that with "he was in a hurry," we have entered the realm of speculation and myth.

Side and end up having a son, Jewish, though not Bar Mitz-vahed, whose childhood unfurled over much of the same land-scape, amid the same landmarks and cultural terrain, as J.D. Salinger's.

I am aware that even if my father had lived longer and if I had been old enough to be curious about his life and ask ques-tions — biographers' questions, in a way — I might still have had to rely on other sources. Salinger himself was remarkably unforthcoming about his wartime experiences with his own daughter. My father's older brother survived him for many years, and every now and then I would launch a charm offensive and try to get my uncle to give me some facts about that time in Vienna; I never got much.

Once, trying to set the scene, I asked if my father, preparing to flee Vienna by train, had packed socks. I was trying to figure out what it was like. Was it like packing for a weekend? Or a sin-gle night? Or was his only baggage the bag of apples he took on the train?

To me this question was an attempt to connect with that moment on a human scale. It was, in a roundabout way, a Sal-ingerian device — emphasizing the superficial surface in such a way that one can sense, by juxtaposition, the activity at much greater depths. My uncle did not see it as such. He thought the question was trivializing. Not that he put it in those words. What he said, in that way his temper would abruptly flare and he would become not loud but the opposite, quiet and very cold, was, "Socks? You're asking about socks? Do you have any idea of the despair with which such a trip would be taken?"

Salinger's Viennese experience is documented in a highly au-tobiographical story, "A Girl I Knew," which Salinger wrote in 1946–1947. The narrator of the story, John, is an especially cal-low rich kid who flunks out of college and then has to confront his parents' respective reactions to this news: The father wants to send him to Europe to learn the family business; the mother is still rehashing the events of the calamity, tacking against the winds of culpability toward the far-off shore of her son's innocence. She laments that he should have gone to see his faculty adviser. "That was what he was there for," she says, as though the school had somehow dropped the ball. I think of a note in Salinger's McBurney file — Jerry has been hit with a medicine ball (meaning, in all likelihood, that he failed to catch it) and his mother wants to know: "Why was there not adequate supervision?"

John's reaction to the father's edict is eye-rolling disgust at the thought of working for his father combined with a curiously impassive amenability. "When the familiar moment came for me to advance one of my fragile promises *really* to apply myself this time," says the narrator, "I let it go by unused."

I suspect this was Salinger's response as well. He knew what he wanted to do, but he needed time to unravel himself to the point where he could do it. This was his bid for time, and a chance to get out from under his father's disapproving gaze.

13

"A Girl I Knew"

H ERB KAUFFMAN, A close friend of Salinger's from Valley Forge, spent one autumn living at the Salingers' apartment and often joined the family for dinner, where he had a front-row seat at the frosty relations between father and son.

"Sol Salinger was not at all 'sensitive' in the way Jerome D. Salinger believed himself to be. Sol just didn't want his son to be a writer."[1]

Jerry had no respect for his father's business and the business, via the men who ran it, reciprocated the sentiment. In "A Girl I Knew," John reports that one obstacle to his father's plan is "I happened to give both his partners the willies on sight."

---

1 The clause "believed himself to be" is a little grenade of hostility. Was there a falling-out? The odds seem high, given that if Kauffman had still been close to Salinger he would not have corresponded with Hamilton. Salinger alludes to Kauffman three times in letters to Elizabeth Murray written between 1946 and 1954. Each reference cascades a bit further into a feeling that, in typical Salinger style, is not one pure thing but rather a distillation of several, in this case a disappointment shading into contempt. He bumps into a hatless Kauffman on Madison Avenue, and recounts the exchange as though a civilized man, Salinger, has been confronted with a degenerate figure who was once his friend, but has now joined the ranks of men without hats. Kauffman depresses him, yet he refuses to share any backward glances with his old friend — the one whose facsimile stands before him.

About Sol's old colleagues in the cheese trade on Harrison Street in Tribeca, Hamilton wrote: "Mostly Italian. Strong dynastic flavor. Many Antolinis."

The name rings out—Mr. Antolini, Holden's old teacher, lives on Sutton Place and lets him sleep on the couch; Holden wakes at dawn to find Mr. Antolini petting his head. If it's not quite a molestation it is close, and perhaps the creepiest scene in the book.

"Probably for every man there is at least one city that sooner or later turns into a girl. How well or how badly the man actually knew the girl doesn't necessarily affect the transformation. She was there, and she was the whole city, and that's that."

In "A Girl I Knew," the girl that is Vienna is named Leah, the beautiful daughter of John's host family. "I met Leah in a nice way," he reports, and the line foreshadows the comically chaste, blushing aspect of the relationship, which mostly centers on the two young people sitting in John's room, listening to one of his two records and practicing their respective second languages:

> "Uh. *Waren Sie heute in der Kino?*" was a favorite question of mine. (Did you go to the movies today?) Five days a week Leah worked in her father's cosmetics plant.
>
> "No. I was today working by my fahzzer."
>
> "Oh, *dass ist recht!* Uh. *Ist es schön dort?*" (Oh, that's right. Is it nice there?)
>
> "No. It is a very big fabric, with very many people running around about."
>
> "Oh. *Dass ist schlecht.*" (That's bad.)

There is a fraught encounter out in the world, in a movie theater lobby, where John meets Leah's fiancé. It bears a strong resemblance to a scene in *Catcher,* which first appeared in his 1941 story "Slight Rebellion off Madison," in which Holden stands around a theater lobby with Sally Hayes, who is talking to some loathsome phonies about the actors. My thought about this is that either Salinger had a very strong affection for scenes in theater lobbies, or that maybe people used to spend much more time talking and socializing in theater lobbies than they do now.

Before John leaves Vienna there is the memorable line, another of his excellent throwaways: "A man can't go along indefinitely carrying around in his pocket a key that doesn't fit anything."

Years later, after the war, John returns to 18 Stiefel Street and has a long confrontation with an apathetic staff sergeant who, "sitting at an Army desk on the first landing, cleaning his fingernails," won't let him upstairs. The enemy is the insufferable bureaucracy of the army. Leah's fate hangs in the balance as he moves through this ghost building, seeking to literally enter a room from his past.

The Bacon King

IN THE TOWN OF BYDGOSZCZ, in north-central Po-
land, there is a plaque featuring the likeness of J.D. Salinger
on the side of a redbrick shopping center. A committee of
local boosters had initially planned for a whole statue of Salinger — to be located in a field of rye, no less — but they ran out of
money. So now there is a plaque that was paid for by the owner
of the shopping center, which in a past life was a slaughterhouse.

After Vienna, Salinger had proceeded to this small Polish
town, where Solomon had secured a job for him in the business
of Poland's Bacon King, Oskar Robinson. There was a hiccup
in the plan so morbid it's almost funny: Between the time Solomon made arrangements for his son to work for Robinson and
his son's arrival to start work, Robinson had dropped dead in
a Viennese casino. Still, there was work to be done. And that
work involved that other word for "ham," the word you use if
the ham is alive: "pigs."

For a time Salinger would make a predawn appearance at
the giant pen where the pigs were slaughtered. The foreman,
who was his guide and immediate superior, had a reputation
for enjoying the psychological torture of his animals, walking
around and firing a handgun into the overhead lights above the
soon-to-be-slaughtered pigs. The report of the handgun going
off would surely have elicited Salinger's distress, distaste. Did
little shards of glass sprinkle down like confetti upon the frantic

animals? There is nothing to attest to this, other than the logic of the action and its consequence.

"For a brief while he went out with a man at four o'clock in the morning and bought and sold pigs," William Maxwell, a friend from *The New Yorker,* would later recall in his write-up in advance of the publication of *The Catcher in the Rye.* I have tremendous respect for William Maxwell but must point out the gentleness with which he offers the image. Salinger, not one for gore, was more direct in the contributor's note that *Story* magazine ran alongside his short story "Once a Week Won't Kill You" in 1944. "I was supposed to apprentice myself to the Polish ham business. They finally dragged me off to Bydgoszcz for a couple of months, where I slaughtered pigs, wagoned through the snow with the big slaughter-master."

15

The Eighth-Grade Canon

I WAS INTRODUCED to J.D. Salinger in the eighth grade by a committed and intense teacher named Larry Colan. His syllabus comprised what I think of as the eighth-grade canon: *A Separate Peace, To Kill a Mockingbird, 1984, Animal Farm,* and *Lord of the Flies. On the Road*'s author, it turns out, had attended our school's archrival, though Mr. Colan either didn't know this or didn't want to taint his hero with the association. This was at the school that would, a few years later, ask me to leave.

Mr. Colan had a beard but no mustache. He was on the short side but had broad shoulders and a strong build. I recall him moving down the hallway holding a brimming cup of hot coffee out in front of him, taking careful and very steady steps, focusing on the coffee as though it were a bomb. He was a coffee and cigarettes man. When he talked about books it was life and death. Outside the classroom, he had a propensity for accidents. An aura of intensity with a hint of violence surrounded him. I recall the time he came to class and informed us he had broken a tooth over the weekend while playing touch football. "I was focusing on the ball, and the man covering me was focusing on the ball," he said. It seemed profound at the time.

About twenty-five years later I went to visit him.

He was mostly unchanged, the Lincolnesque beard still present, his body still athletic, stocky, stoic, and breaking down all at once. There was a stylish black-and-white photograph of him up on the wall in which he regards the camera with a slight smile and a very black eye.

The feeling I had of his being some kind of Dostoyevskian figure hiding out in the basement was more intense. He spoke of the desire of the school to appease parents with maximum transparency about what goes on in his class, what the assignments are — all of this information to be made available online — and how he was resisting it. As ever, it seemed to be a losing battle but one he was committed to fighting. I felt a glimmer of the old enthusiasm I had for him, similar to what the kids in "The Laughing Man" feel for the Chief. He is someone who would fight for you.

The details of our conversations from that day about *The Catcher in the Rye* elude me. The standout memory of that eighth-grade class, besides the intensity and physical presence of Mr. Colan himself, was our discussion of *On the Road*. He asked us to describe how it was written. I raised my hand. "It's like," I began, but the thought vanished, and I started loudly drumming a beat on the desk. I was faltering. I recall a sadness coming over me. I thought I had something to say.

"Exactly," said Mr. Colan. "Do that again!"

"Do what?"

"Drum on the desk."

I drummed.

"Exactly!"

I wrote, or tried to write, my first stories for Mr. Colan sitting before an ominously humming IBM Selectric typewriter. Its fierce little typeball smacked the paper with such force that every letter was like a gunshot; a sentence was strafing machine-gun fire. The whole experience with Mr. Colan was percussive, a series of impacts. This extended to the reading list — it crashed into you. It's strange to think of all those books now, and the ways in which they do or do not echo one another. *A Separate*

Peace has some cosmetic similarities with *The Catcher in the Rye* in terms of milieu and prep school setting, but that book is about a friendship, and Holden doesn't really have friends, or if he does there is no illusion that they can really help him, even if they wanted to, which they don't.[1] His relationships are elsewhere, nowhere, and with himself.

A few years after my visit to Mr. Colan, a woman approached me after a reading and said she was Mr. Colan's sister. We had a nice chat and I told her to send him my regards. Her face changed. In hindsight it's amazing how long it took for me to grasp its meaning.

"You don't know?" she said.

It turns out he had killed himself. Thankfully, she didn't say how.

"I'm so sorry," she said.

"I'm so sorry," I said.

"I am so sorry to tell you like that."

"How are you supposed to tell me?"

We stood there for a minute saying sorry to each other while I flashed back to the time I maneuvered a small bright reflection off my watch and onto his back, where it hovered tremulously, now and then sliding off him and onto the blackboard next to where he was writing, and how after a while without turning around he yelled, "Quit it, Beller!" And I did. Somehow I took his certainty that it was me as a compliment.

---

1 An accidental echo of one of my favorite lines in *The Catcher in the Rye,* when Ackley insists that he brushes his teeth. "No, you don't," Holden replies. "I've seen you, and you don't."

16

The Muse of Manasquan

IN THE SUMMER OF 1938, Salinger's friend Bill Faison from Valley Forge brought Salinger over to his sister's house in Brielle, on the Jersey Shore. There he met one of the more significant figures in his development as a writer, Elizabeth Murray.

We find our mentors in many places other than school, and education happens on many levels, including the sentimental one. Many of the teachers in a person's life are not educators or even mentors. They are friends, but also coconspirators of a sort, working on a project together. If you are playing the younger student role, that project is you.

Such was the dynamic between Salinger and Elizabeth Murray. She was twice his age, knew about literature, and seemed happy to have this younger male friend the same age as her son.

Murray was a vivacious, charismatic woman, with a wide circle of friends that included Agnes O'Neill, who was raising her daughter with Eugene O'Neill, Oona, on her own in the next town up the Jersey Shore. Murray was not an artist herself but someone who knew about art and moved in that world. She had kept her wits, and her family, together through several enormous setbacks.

I can't help thinking of her as a figure out of Fitzgerald, perched somewhere between the gaiety of *This Side of Paradise* and the much more somber, aching tone of *Tender Is the Night.*

Murray would have been among that famous generation of flappers whom Fitzgerald illuminated and to some extent modeled. And it was Murray who encouraged Salinger, shortly after they met in 1938, to read F. Scott Fitzgerald.

A friendship such as this is charged by a kind of erotics of patronage. Dancers, painters, musicians have them. Athletes have them all the time. I sometimes think this is why coaches are so notoriously abrasive and obnoxious — this is always rationalized as a means for motivating players but I think it's also a way to extinguish any sense of tenderness that could be misconstrued.

The motivations of these benevolent mentors always seem benign, and at the same time a feeling of need, of ulterior motive — sexual or romantic in nature — is undeniable even if it is never acted upon or even thought about consciously.[1]

When Salinger met Murray she had just returned from the most recent of her marital fiascos. The first, and most tragic, occurred nineteen years earlier when her husband died in a plane crash. He was flying the plane in a training exercise. She was pregnant at the time and had a son, John. She later got engaged to a man with a faintly gangsterish air about him. No one in Murray's family knew exactly what he did. He lived in the Bahamas and gave her an engagement ring with a giant diamond. Murray's family never found out what he did because at the last moment she called off the wedding. Her fiancé insisted she keep the ring. A gesture of friendship, I was told, not of spite.

Murray later married Adie Murray, a Scotsman, and she

---

1 I had someone like this in my life, a lovely if somewhat strange man who came to my small-time college basketball games and often sat next to my mother, who was always happy enough for the company if a little confused as to who he was. I met him, or he met me, when he volunteered some advice on post moves on the basketball court of the McBurney YMCA, on West Sixty-Third Street.

moved to Scotland with him. They had a daughter, Gloria,[2] after whom Salinger would ask with fondness in letters that spanned over two decades. The marriage didn't last; Adie was an abusive alcoholic. She moved back to New Jersey.

When Jerry Salinger met her, Murray was living with her daughter in a big house in Brielle, four blocks from the Manasquan post office and about a mile from the ocean. She had cousins in Staten Island and went up frequently to visit, and from there would sometimes travel to Greenwich Village to hang out in cafés with her young friend the aspiring writer. He would read her his stories in progress. They would talk about literature and, inevitably, Salinger's bright future role in it.

In his letters to her, he shares personal news, asks after her, engages in all the gestures of friendship. But mostly he reports on his progress toward their shared goal — his success as a writer.

---

2 When Murray sold her cache of Salinger letters she was well aware that it was a betrayal of enormous proportions, and to this day her family is, if not exactly ambivalent about it, still working through the issue. Her great-granddaughter Sarah Norris published an interesting account of how the family talks about the sale — the key rationalizing detail being that Elizabeth had used the proceeds to send Gloria to college. She was going to have to sell the letters or that diamond ring from the gangster. The letters were worth more. Gloria later sold the ring to help finance a house.

1938: "The Young Man Went Back to College"

Once there was a young man who was tired of trying to grow a moustache. This same young man did not want to go to work for his Daddykins — or any other unreasonable man. So the young man went back to college.

— J.D.S., *Ursinus Weekly,* October 10, 1938

I N MARCH 1938 Jerry Salinger returned home from Europe to 1133 Park Avenue. To say his interest in joining his father's business had not been piqued by his European experience is probably an understatement, though it's also hard to imagine he could have been any less enthusiastic about it than he was when he left.

So Salinger did what many young people do when unsure of what to do next: He went back to school. Ursinus College, a small liberal arts college outside of Philadelphia, was founded in 1869 by the German Reformed Church. Its emphasis was on prelaw, medicine, and chemistry. Most of the students were industrious, local, and they expected to be smiled at when passing a fellow student on a campus walk.

The most generous interpretation as to how he ended up there is to speculate on whether Colonel Baker of nearby Valley Forge Military Academy played some role. The least gener-

ous — and totally speculative — interpretation is that Solomon
Salinger was as interested in his son getting a crash course in assimilation as he was in anything else — it certainly was a place
where J.D. Salinger had the urbane, moody, Jewish New Yorker
role entirely to himself.

Ian Hamilton, industrious master of the cold-calling letter, wrote to Salinger's Ursinus classmates. Quite a few wrote
back. Their responses are imbued with the interesting tension
of an unresolved story. Salinger had been seriously famous for
over three decades by then. Yet he had not published anything
new in so long that he was likely fading into an abstraction.
His saga was unfinished, suspended. His classmates' testimo-
nies are tinged with both a fondness that veers toward eulogy
and a sense of irritation that such a foreign, unappealing figure
should, by virtue of his success, somehow speak for their school.

"It was a good, basic liberal arts college, its smallness contributed to closeness of students and professors," wrote one
classmate. "However, not always. The 'not always' included
Jerry Salinger."

Another classmate recalled: "Although we talked on several
occasions, I can not remember why Jerry Salinger came to such
a school. It seemed evident to me he was bored and unhappy."

Yet another classmate wrote: "Jerry came from New York
and looked on college and the students with disdain. He seemed
so dissatisfied . . . He never smiled, gave a friendly greeting or responded to overtures of acceptance. His manner was nasty. His
remarks, if any, were caustic."

Ian Hamilton cites all the respondents in a group footnote
and doesn't say which were girls and which were boys. But it's
not hard to infer.

"Jerry Salinger was tall, slender, with dark hair and eyes,"
wrote one classmate. "He had an olive complexion. His hands
were long fingered and sensitive. The nails were bitten short

and were tobacco stained. He smiled infrequently but seemed almost mischievous when he did."

Another reported: "When this handsome, suave and sophisticated New Yorker in the black chesterfield coat (complete with velvet collar) hit campus in 1938, we had never seen anything quite like it. We were enchanted by his biting and acerbic manner, and his writing in the weekly publication we found hilarious and always devastatingly on target."

"The girls were impressed by Jerry's good looks — tall, dark, and handsome — and we were in awe of his New York City background and worldly ways. Of course, there were other handsome men on campus — I married one. But Jerry was different, a loner, a critic, not one of the crowd. The boys, incidentally, were not impressed by or in awe of Jerry Salinger. My husband was not too kind just now when I asked him how he felt about Ursinus's claim to fame. His avowed purpose in life was to become a famous writer, and he declared openly that he would one day produce the Great American Novel. Jerry and I became special friends, mostly I am sure, because I was the only one who believed he would do it. He felt that his English professors at Ursinus were more interested in how he dotted his i's and crossed his t's than they were in developing his literary style."

The author of this last note is Frances Thierolf, who later married a man named Glassmoyer. Salinger wrote to Frances saying that Glassmoyer was the funniest name he had ever heard. "He promised to write a book about me," she wrote, "and while I claim not the slightest resemblance to Franny Glass, the name did seem like something of a coincidence."

Salinger's separateness from his classmates extended to his living quarters, which were a bit surreal.

"I roomed in what was then known as Freeland Hall," a classmate wrote, "a properly ancient building which accommodated the kitchen and dining halls in the basement and first floors and rooms on the second and third floors, and, I believe, only one small room in the attic or bell tower. That is where JDS lived alone. It is my recollection that he was the bell ringer."

You have no say about your freshman dorm room, just as you have no say about the home in which you grow up, though it's possible that during a transition one can chime in with an opinion and exert some influence. About the era that is the setting for your youth, you have no say at all.

The 1930s were a decade that saw the emergence of hard-boiled detective stories as hugely popular entertainment. "Poets of tabloid murder," Edmund Wilson called them.

In the early years of the Depression, writes Morris Dickstein in *Dancing in the Dark,* his cultural history of the 1930s, "the individual was usually shown either as a victim, as in *I Am a Fugitive from a Chain Gang,* or as an aggressive loner, as in the classic gangster films of 1930–32 or the hard-boiled novels of Dashiell Hammett, such as *Red Harvest, The Maltese Falcon,* or *The Glass Key.*"

The existential flavor of this writing coexisted with a highly pragmatic one — these books were written to sell. Salinger absorbed this, too. The stories he would later sell to the slicks (*Collier's, Saturday Evening Post, Good Housekeeping*) were part of becoming "a professional." He wanted to get paid, and he was an artist of the highest purpose. One of his accomplishments was integrating these two wishes into a single voice.

Salinger lasted a total of nine weeks at Ursinus, but those weeks contained significant clues to his influences. During this time he wrote a column for the school newspaper, "Musings of a Social Soph: The Skipped Diploma." He wrote a total of nine columns, the first appearing on October 10, 1938. Composed mostly of batty snippets in the style of *The New Yorker*'s Notes and Comment section of the day, the column is juvenile, debonair, and contemptuous, with the occasional flash of Salinger's playful, at times malevolent, humor.

Examples:

Letter:
Dear Mother — You and your husband have failed to raise me properly. I can neither Begin the Beguin [*sic*] nor identify Joe Oglemurphey's torrid trumpet. In short, college life for me is not too peachy — Dolefully yours, Phoebe Phrosh

Lovelorn Dept.:
Question — I go with a boy who is so very confusing. Last Wednesday night I refused to kiss him good-night, and he became very angry. For nearly ten minutes he screamed at the top of his voice. Then suddenly he hit me full in the mouth with his fist. Yet, he says he loves me. What am I to think???
Answer — Remember, dearie. No one is perfect. Love is strange and beautiful. Ardor is to be admired. Have you tried kissing him?

Campus Dept.:
It was all a mistake. They were alumni. They have never even been to Mars.

Memorandum:
There are only sixty-nine more shopping-days. Do it early this year.

And this entry from his column on October 10:

Reflection:
It all links . . .
Men bore me;
Women abhor me;
Children floor me;
Society stinks . . .

This snippet may be revealing of Salinger's own state of mind, but it is undoubtedly revealing about his literary influences and models. One can hear the rhythm and mood of Dorothy Parker's famous poem "Resumé," which ends:

> *Guns aren't lawful;*
> *Nooses give;*
> *Gas smells awful;*
> *You might as well live.*

Parker was part of the Algonquin Round Table, a group of wits who became associated with *The New Yorker* and its early success. Other members included Robert Sherwood, Alexander Woollcott, and Robert Benchley. Salinger had already cited Benchley as a role model as far back as his Valley Forge years. All of these figures would go on to be strongly identified with the magazine. But they were not made by *The New Yorker; The New Yorker* was, to an extent, made by them.

The New Yorker

I don't want to hear about it.

— HAROLD ROSS

AROLD ROSS FOUNDED *The New Yorker* and edited it for its first twenty-seven years, during which
time Salinger made his debut in the magazine and
became strongly identified with it, and yet Ross's greatest influence on Salinger may have occurred long before Salinger's writing ever appeared in its pages.

Ross was born in Aspen, Colorado, in 1892. When the sil-
ver mine that was the town's economic foundation went bust a
few years later his father, a grocer, moved the family to Salt Lake
City. While his father eked out a living, Ross got involved in the
high school paper — though he wasn't yet in high school — and
started freelancing for the *Salt Lake Tribune.* At age thirteen he
ran away from home, all the way to Denver, where he worked
briefly for the *Denver Post,* and though he eventually returned
home, he never went back to school. He got a job at another
local newspaper and soon was bouncing from city to city and
newspaper to newspaper throughout the American West with
such frequency that his friends called him "the Hobo." His location was inconsistent but his trade was not: He was a news-

paperman. In the memorable words of his friend Herbert Asbury, author of *The Gangs of New York,* "He could not only get it. He could write it."

The Hobo would eventually found *The New Yorker* in 1925. His biography is aptly called *Genius in Disguise.*

The New Yorker was a humor magazine first and foremost. The juxtaposition of this self-educated rube running arguably the most sophisticated magazine in America was ridiculous, and the ridiculous was an essential part of the magazine's humor. "American nonsense wit," as Wilfrid Sheed put it. This kind of humor wasn't a joke, exactly, and could not be unpacked, or delivered, as such. It was a sound. Ross could hear this sound in his head but he struggled to get it on the pages of his magazine. *The New Yorker*'s first couple of years were dominated by Ross's frantic search to find writers who could play that tune. He finally did find them in E.B. White and James Thurber, and things developed from there.

Yet Ross was never quite satisfied. His restless, agitated search for people to add to the orchestra, and to fine-tune its sound, became part of the sound itself. His magazine made an art of mocking bourgeois complacency in the service of enabling it — a similar homeopathic mechanism that makes *The Catcher in the Rye* such a popular tool for socializing adolescents.[1]

Ross's byline never appeared in the magazine — but then

---

1 Its effect is homeopathic because, as Louis Menand wrote with typical acuity, "*The Catcher in the Rye* is a sympathetic portrait of a boy who refuses to be socialized which has become ... a standard instrument of socialization. I was introduced to the book by my parents, people who, if they had ever imagined that I might, after finishing the thing, run away from school, smoke like a chimney, lie about my age in bars, solicit a prostitute, or use the word 'goddam' in every third sentence, would (in the words of the story) have had about two hemorrhages apiece. Somehow, they knew this wouldn't be the effect."

hardly did anyone else's. It's amazing how few bylines popu-
lated the magazine in its first decades, and how demurely se-
creted away are the few that do appear, but his somewhat bray-
ing and overly loud voice permeates every syllable and cartoon.
He is probably the only editor who is famous for a margin note
with which he would often query pieces of both fact and fiction: "Who that?"

Ross had a direct influence on Salinger. He hired the editors
whose pencils marked up Salinger's stories, among them Katharine White, William Maxwell, Gustave Lobrano, and William Shawn. He approved the purchase of Salinger's first story,
"Slight Rebellion off Madison," in 1941. He was surely part of
the last-minute decision to delay publishing it after the attack
on Pearl Harbor. He pops up in 1946, when the magazine did
finally publish it, and again in January 1948, when *The New
Yorker* published "A Perfect Day for Bananafish."

Ross and Salinger were both present in the soon-to-be-de-
molished Ritz-Carlton at the magazine's glittering, champagne-
soaked twenty-fifth anniversary party in 1950, a capstone event
for Ross and the magazine in ways that no one at that party
could have anticipated. Salinger was living in New York at the
time, in his own apartment, and was, in Roger Angell's words, "a
star."

When Ross was in the hospital in 1951, Salinger wrote him
a warm letter wishing him to get well, sharing personal news,
and signing off, with his typical flair for awkwardness, "contri-
butionally."

Ross recovered, and wrote to Salinger inviting him out to
his country house. "I'll put you down for the spring... If you
should want to come earlier than that, let me know, for my present plan is to keep the joint open for winter." But Ross didn't
live through the winter.

———

Harold Ross was the patriarch of the family into which Salinger was so happy to be adopted. Given the doubts that Salinger's real father had expressed about his writing—though maybe I should say his "professional prospects," since Sol's objections were rooted in pragmatism, not literary criticism—having in Ross a surrogate father who was so supportive of his work would have made him all the more important to Salinger. An irony that was almost certainly unexamined by either was that both men had made distancing themselves from their fathers the first, essential act in the pursuit of their careers.

To understand the interplay of Harold Ross's sensibility on J.D. Salinger, however, one can't focus exclusively on the period of time when Salinger was publishing in *The New Yorker*. Ross's most direct and meaningful influence on Salinger wasn't when Salinger was publishing in Ross's magazine but when he was first reading it. He was among the first generation to grow up with *The New Yorker* lying around as part of the household. I base this observation partly on the Salinger stationery—no name, just *1133 Park Avenue, New York New York* on two lines, in pale gray-blue—whose font is suspiciously reminiscent of *The New Yorker*'s, and partly on the fact that Salinger was citing *New Yorker* writers such as Robert Benchley and Wolcott Gibbs as models as early as his Valley Forge years. His *Ursinus Weekly* column borrows directly in form and tone from *The New Yorker*'s Notes and Comment section. Whether the Salingers subscribed to *The New Yorker* before or after they moved across town in 1932 I do not know, but I feel confident they did and that Salinger grew up imbibing the particular brand of American humor that *The New Yorker* perfected in the 1930s and 1940s via the obsessive energy of Harold Ross. It's significant that one of the last practitioners of this subtle mode of humor, S.J. Perelman, remained close friends with Salinger well into his Cornish seclusion.

When James Thurber published his book *The Years with Ross* in 1959, it created an uproar within *The New Yorker*, with some members feeling Ross had been betrayed and belittled by one of his favorite sons. Salinger drove down from Cornish to join a group that included William Shawn. They met at S.N. Behrman's apartment on Eighty-Eighth Street and Madison Avenue to discuss their fury at Thurber and make plans for a response. Behrman later reported that Salinger, the youngest of the group, was the most upset.

What Salinger produced was a thirty-page essay defending Ross. There is a record of his submitting it to both the *Partisan Review* and the *Saturday Review* in 1960, but neither magazine accepted it and the essay itself has been lost.

"Ross was fascinated by facts and statistics about the big and costly," wrote Thurber in *The Years with Ross*, "but he didn't like his facts bare and stark; he wanted them accompanied by comedy — you unwrapped the laugh and there was a fact, or maybe vice versa."

Thurber's great talent was the depiction of men — in prose and in cartoons — as hapless, thwarted, and pathetic, particularly in their relations with women, and even more particularly with their wives. His most enduring contribution to the culture is "The Secret Life of Walter Mitty." What Thurber did, to some extent, in *The Years with Ross*, was to make Harold Ross into the protagonist of a Thurber cartoon. By the time he wrote it, thirty or so years after he had gone to work for Ross, their relationship was complicated enough to sustain numerous subplots, several of which involved money. Thurber's Ross is constantly portrayed as agitated and frustrated, befuddled, grasping at the controls of his own magazine, which always seemed to elude him. Thurber depicts all this restless agitation as part of his genius, and it rings true, if exaggerated. One moment in particular caught my attention:

> "Men don't mature in this country, Thurber," [Ross] said. "They're children. I was editor of the *Stars and Stripes* when

I was twenty-five. Most men in their twenties don't know their way around yet . . ." He went to the window behind his desk and stared disconsolately down into the street, jingling coins in one of his pants pockets.

According to Thurber, Ross kept five dollars' worth of change in his pocket at all times. The image of the disconsolate, agitated figure, staring abstractedly out the window, his hand moving nervously in his pocket, is an intensely familiar one if you have read J.D. Salinger, in whose work worried, bitten fingers are always being described. A comic nervousness attempting to settle itself down by handling objects emanates from Thurber's portrait of Ross like electricity, and you can hear its echo all over Salinger's work — in Holden's observations about grooming, in the injured fingers of "The Young Folks," "Just Before the War with the Eskimos," and "A Boy in France," in the way Esmé tests the ends of her hair to see if it's dry, in Zooey's bath rituals, in everyone's cigarettes.

The Depression was a halcyon era for magazines and for short story writers in particular. *Esquire* published its first monthly edition on the day Prohibition was repealed, December 5, 1933. It ran a list of its contributors' names on the cover of each issue that first year, with the fiction section featured prominently. One name among the otherwise changing list of contributors under the fiction header — appearing in almost every issue that first year — was F. Scott Fitzgerald.

The 1930s were the decade of the ascendancy of the American short story, not just as an art form but as a commercial proposition — the slicks paid the modern equivalent of $35,000 for a single short story. *Esquire* and *The New Yorker* paid less but in that range.

Esquire's style, and its design, was brazen, masculine, a bit leering. *The New Yorker* had a different attitude. For one thing, it was a bit feminine somehow, more gentle in its mood and tone. It aspired to a mode of sophistication and urbanity. It didn't take on the Depression as an existential question. Its foundational tone was an absurd humor, a kind of music that Salinger, in literary terms, grew up wanting to play.

Roger Angell

S ALINGER has a fantastic ability to get his stories moving quickly. It's a talent that is apparent from the start, yet it shifts to another level, conspicuously more acute and focused, with "A Perfect Day for Bananafish" and in all the stories in *Nine Stories,* seven of which appeared in *The New Yorker.* There is a smell in those stories, a smell of cordite, of a fired gun, something burnt; the smell of omissions, of brush having been cleared. I think it is the smell of really good editing.

It's probably absurd to give editing a smell, though I once walked into Roger Angell's office and said, "It smells the same as it did last time I was here"— however *The New Yorker* had since moved from one building to another.

"What does it smell like?" he said.

"It smells like an old baseball mitt," I said. "Or maybe a horse."

There was a long pause during which, for some reason, I didn't start to take on the possibility that I was deep into the realm of faux pas. Only when he mumbled, "Maybe it's me," did this dawn on me. The moment passed. It was January 1993 and I had last been in his office three years earlier when we worked together side by side on a short story of mine that he said needed only light editing. It was a bitterly cold December morning. When he came to get me in the waiting room he exclaimed, "You should be wearing a coat!"

In his office, he gave me a brief guided tour of the framed photographs. This, I grasped, was part history lesson and part family album — Ann Beattie in the company of *The New Yorker* editor Chip McGrath was in one photo; in another was Roger's young son, not too much younger than I; in another was an old, stodgy man squinting out through a smile, wearing a tie. "V.S. Pritchett," said Roger. "He only just now stopped writing. He's about ninety-two. Said he couldn't keep it together anymore."

Then he told me to pull my chair around next to his so we could both look at the manuscript on his desk. There was my familiar dot matrix printout, with his penciled notation on nearly every line. When, on the third page, I finally challenged a particular edit, a comma inserted or removed, he said, "Okay."

"Okay? Really?"

"It's your story."

"Huh. In that case, can we start again from the beginning?"

Roger Angell is legendary at *The New Yorker* for many things. Being warm and cuddly is not among them. Back when I first met him, when he was seventy-two, I heard that he was known around the office for being able to jump from a standing position up onto a table. I wasn't told if this was a historic feat of athleticism or if he was still prone to doing it. I didn't rule the latter out.

Now, at ninety-three, he is a fiction editor whose rejection letters are so artful, insightful, and devastating they should perhaps be collected, and he contributes regularly to the magazine (and blogs) as he has for six decades, going back to the late 1940s.

A year or so earlier I had been in the magazine's offices to record a podcast. Afterward I had been led to Roger's office, where I thought we had a plan to say hi, but he wasn't there. He had left the light on and no one was sure if he had just stepped away or was gone for the day. It felt as though something urgent had called him away and he had left in a rush.

I had been reluctant to communicate with him and send things in for so long. I had been so circumspect. Is it coyness or a fear of disappointing that makes one so reticent with those who have been generous with you, especially editors? Finally I was going to come in to say hello, be personable. But was I too late? A melodrama played out in my mind.

It was a cold winter day when I came in to talk about Salinger. That empty office had been poignant; the office with him in it was poignant, too. Roger still had it together. He received me with another photo tour. He showed me a photograph of William Trevor, who Roger said had a story coming up, which I take to mean a story that he had edited. There was a beautiful black-and-white photograph of John Updike in profile at the end of a golf swing.

"Updike had a perfect golf swing. Perfect," muttered Roger. The topic of golf evokes a side of Updike that I find unappealing, something smug and religious in its sense of perfection that has cloyingly reactionary overtones for me; yet I also had my first feeling of warmth toward the game via an essay of Roger's that appeared in his book *Let Me Finish*,[1] in which he recalled being a young man stealing a quick round one morning in the company of a young woman who somehow loses her engagement ring on the course, which he then tries to help her find.

"What's that?" I said, pointing to a large photograph taped to the window, partially obscuring the view of an office building directly across Forty-Second Street. "It looks familiar."

---

1 The old American Nonsense Humor Orchestra strikes up with the image summoned by this title: a man at the head of a table full of people, his hand raised, trying to corral everyone's wandering attention, faintly ridiculous in his efforts and also inoculated against ridiculousness by virtue of his drawing attention to it, a fundamental bit of *New Yorker* jujitsu whose movements Roger both inherited and further developed.

"It's the view from my old office," said Roger. "I like it better."

I looked more closely at the picture and saw Bryant Park and the back of the New York Public Library as seen from his old office, a block and a half east of where we now sat.

Roger put his leg up on a chair. We discussed the fact that *The New Yorker* would be moving, along with all the other Condé Nast magazines, to a new place down in Battery Park City in a couple of years. "I don't think I will make that move," he said. "It will be great for everyone coming from Brooklyn but it's too far from where I live."

He lives on the Upper East Side, a few blocks from where he grew up; both the childhood home and the current one are just a couple blocks away from 1133 Park Avenue. We talked about Salinger for a while. When going for cigarettes as a teenager, or a man in his twenties, I wondered, which way would he go — up the hill to Madison or down the hill to Lexington? Roger offered a disquisition on the nature and character of the two avenues in those years, and thought it likely Salinger would have gone up the hill to Madison Avenue. He then described his memory of the magazine's twenty-fifth anniversary party in 1950, which he and Salinger both attended. "He was just another writer," said Roger. "He was a star, no question about it, but the atmosphere of holiness and mystery wasn't there."

I flashed briefly on some of the other outsize personalities who would have been in attendance: Harold Ross, for starters, and E.B. White and James Thurber, and the relatively recently arrived luminaries like A.J. Liebling and Joseph Mitchell, two very different sides of the same coin, not to mention all the journalists whose names are now partly obscured by time but on whose work the magazine's reputation had been built: St. Clair McKelway, Geoffrey Hellman, Joel Sayre, Janet Flanner, John McNulty. Would the surviving Algonquinites — Dorothy Parker, Wolcott Gibbs — have been there, too? Probably. Must have been quite a party.

Among the circulating crowd would have been Katharine White, who was *The New Yorker*'s first fiction editor, hired in 1925. "She knows the Bible, and literature, and foreign languages," Harold Ross told Thurber on the day the two men met. "And she has taste." She was also Roger Angell's mother. She left his father for E.B. White.

"Do you think Salinger learned something about writing by being edited by your mother and other *New Yorker* editors?" I asked.

Roger shrugged, the discomfort of the gesture indicative, perhaps, of his distaste for the encroachment of touchy-feely subject matter.

"But don't you think a writer learns about writing by the way they are edited? I mean if it's a good editor? Because Salinger's stories after he started publishing in *The New Yorker* are different in some way from what came before. Don't you think you learned from whoever first edited you here? I mean, about both writing and editing?"

"I didn't learn from being edited," Roger said. "I had been around writers and editors my whole life. I saw my mother working at the kitchen table with pencils and manuscripts when I was five years old."

I thought of a line by the critic Nancy Franklin in her piece about Katharine White: "As an editor she was maternal, and as a mother, she was editorial."

Roger's only further comment on Salinger was, "For the record, I don't think he was writing anything up there. Or rather he may have been writing but it's not writing unless you show it to someone. Writing is meant to be read. It's in dialogue with the reader. If there is no reader it's not writing."

This I took home with me and mulled over for a while. No matter how much I thought about it I could not really agree.

I wrote Roger:

I am still pondering your remark that whatever Salinger was doing up in his bunker it wasn't writing, because writing is for a reader. It's a very provocative remark. I have since come up with all sorts of retorts — what about Kafka, and Emily Dickinson? What if he left a note saying, "publish this in a hundred years"?

Roger responded:

If "Always think of the reader" is by far the best advice to urge upon a beginning writer it's because it confirms that writing is communication above all; what you're putting down is meant to be seen and absorbed by somebody else. It's a two-way process. I don't care much about Dickinson or Kafka, because they're so clearly the exception. Whenever I myself start writing something to myself it quickly loses interest and rarely shows any quality.

The Professional

The first semester at Columbia, Salinger just
looked out the window. The second semester,
he continued to look out the window.

— WHIT BURNETT

I N JANUARY 1939, Jerry Salinger went back to school.
But he was no longer a college student, at least not techni-
cally. I encountered, in his other biographies, the sentence
"He enrolled at Columbia University." Perhaps this is correct
in the most narrow, technical sense, but it would be like looking up at the wall in a doctor's office and seeing a Harvard diploma, only to discover, on closer inspection, that it is a certificate that indicates the doctor took a single course in Harvard
night school. In Salinger's case he was enrolled in what Columbia University then called "University Extension" and now calls
"the School of General Studies."

Then, as now, the students were an amalgam of adults who
wanted to pursue an interest in writing, a smattering of Columbia undergraduates, and an assortment of youthful refugees whose previous adventures in academia had not gone well,
and who were now in a kind of purgatory. This is the group to
which J.D. Salinger belonged.

The teachers of University Extension, then and now, were not Columbia professors but adjuncts — practicing writers and editors. Some were preoccupied with their main line of work and a bit detached in their teaching; some were engaged to an unhealthy degree. Salinger signed up for two courses in the spring semester. He got both extremes.

Charles Hanson Towne was a prolific author who had published copiously in various genres — journalism, plays, novels, poetry. He was effusive, productive, even famous. He had made his way in the tumultuous world of magazine publishing in the early part of the century, working with Theodore Dreiser on the magnificently named *Delineator* (which sounds like a magazine with severe opinions about politics or aesthetics, but was a fashion magazine that printed recipes and knitting patterns), and had edited the *Smart Set,* just before H.L. Mencken and George Jean Nathan took over and made it famous. Towne had edited slicks like *Cosmopolitan* and *Harper's Bazaar.* His most recent book, published in 1939, was the ambiguously titled *Gentlemen Behave: Charles Hanson Towne's Book of Etiquette for Men.* An observation, or a command?

Salinger's world is filled with gentlemen and their youthful antecedents who don't behave, but who nevertheless are sufficiently aware of what behaving might entail that they don't just ignore these strictures — they despise them. And yet, Holden Caulfield's backward hunting cap notwithstanding, Salinger's rebels are hardly showy about it. They are not running around looking like hobos.

Towne's course was in poetry. All of his own poems rhymed. One fragment that might have caught Salinger's eye, or that of any other two-time college dropout:

> *When he went blundering back to God,*
> *His songs half written, his work half done,*

Who knows what paths his bruised feet trod,
What hills of peace or pain he won?

I hope God smiled and took his hand,
And said, "Poor truant, passionate fool!
Life's book is hard to understand:
Why couldst thou not remain at school?"

At the end of Salinger's semester with him, Towne presented Salinger with a special gift: a volume of his own poetry, effusively signed to Salinger as it was no doubt signed to all the other members of the class:

> To Jerome Salinger, for his unfailing attention in the Spring Course, 1939, at Columbia University, from Charles Hanson Towne, New York, May 24: 1939.

Towne kept his students' work. Perhaps he really loved them. Among his papers is a poem by Salinger titled "Early Fall in New York." It gives every indication as to why Salinger would leave no other trace of poetry, but it also takes a wonderful swerve into sex at the end. After rhyming couplets about leaves and then the sun, the narrator comes upon — with the surprise of an innocent wandering the brambles — a bevy of nude ladies.

The narrator comments on their attractive mink. There is no reference to a coat, or anything else, just that one suggestive word, "mink." The poem finishes the couplet by finding a rhyming word for "ladies" that is a Greek word for hell. The finale consists of three lines that announce the narrator's love for the women's hard heels. "Hard" is repeated.

Like some fascinating prehistoric fossil form, these phrases suggest a deep engagement with the city and its sounds and atmosphere, and also a raw, youthful wish for a sexual encounter in Central Park. What is missing here is the patina of wistfulness. It is not worked over and burnished with that feeling of longing that is part of Holden Caulfield's voice. Instead there is a note of sex, punishment, and appreciation — themes that would be conspicuous in the first panel of the Salinger triptych, which was about to commence.

Room 505

WHIT BURNETT'S COURSE was called "Professional Writing." The course description read: "For professional writers who wish constructive criticism, assistance with their individual problems, and the stimulus of regular work with a small group of writers."

It met on Mondays from 7:30 to 9:10 p.m. in room 505 of a building on the Columbia campus called, at the time, "Business," now named Dodge Hall, the first building to your left as you enter the main gate at Broadway and 116th Street. To get to room 505 Salinger had to climb two flights of broad black stairs that turn back at the landing halfway between every flight. Anyone would be winded at the top of this climb. Salinger, like Holden Caulfield, was a heavy smoker. He would sit in the back of Burnett's class and smoke continuously. Joining him back there was Mrs. Sterling. She was the oldest member of the class, and often wrote about forsythias. Now and then she would chastise the young man beside her for smoking too much.

Whatever stimulus Salinger received from Burnett's instruction, its effect was hard to discern in the first semester that Salinger took his class. He contributed nothing in the way of work or comment, but he came to class, sitting in the back, smoking, and looking out the window. He took the class again the following fall of 1939. He may have taken the class to keep his father off his back. Or maybe he thought Burnett had something to offer.

Burnett was editor and cofounder, with his wife, Martha Foley, of *Story* magazine, which by 1939 had established itself as a kind of legend. He had a talent for spotting talent. One of the most important measures of a literary editor's value is how many interesting voices he discovers. By this metric Burnett is one of the greats. William Saroyan, James Purdy, Truman Capote, Carson McCullers, Norman K. Mailer (as his byline appeared at the time), and Joseph Heller all had their debuts in his magazine. And though today's young writers often read and write about these authors as peers, it's striking to note that Burnett published early work by not one but two pillars of the eighth-grade canon—John Knowles, author of *A Separate Peace,* and Salinger.

"A very modest man who had a beautiful white goatee" is how Norman Mailer described him circa 1941, after he won *Story*'s college fiction contest and just two years after Salinger had Burnett as a teacher. Writing in the early 1970s, Mailer called Burnett "a legend," and said of *Story,* "young writers in the late thirties and the years of the Second World War used to dream of appearing in its pages about the way a young rock group might feel transcendent in these hours with the promise of a spread in *Rolling Stone.*"

In spite of this, or maybe because of it, Salinger could hardly be bothered to pay attention to the man with the white goatee. Instead, he spent a lot of time staring out the window.

Burnett's teaching style was not exactly avid; he was a conspicuously undemonstrative figure, raised as a Mormon in Salt Lake City by a mother who, his daughter suspects, was from the Ute tribe. When the Church of Jesus Christ of Latter-day Saints asked him to go abroad to proselytize, he said he would agree to do it if it sent him to Barcelona. The church declined. Burnett went to Europe on his own and became a journalist. For a period of time he ran a newspaper called the *Paris Herald*. His nickname was "Surly and Sour Burnett."

Salinger wrote an appraisal of Burnett in 1964; it didn't see print until after Burnett's death, when his second wife and coeditor, Hallie Burnett, used it as an afterword to her *Fiction Writer's Handbook* in 1975. By 1964 Salinger and Burnett's relationship had undergone many complications. Burnett, who ended up publishing five of Salinger's stories in *Story,* persuaded him just after the war to bring out a collection with Story Press, which was being financed by the publisher J.B. Lippincott. In a pattern that would play out frequently in the postwar years, Burnett, at the time a young editor there, was a fan but the money upstairs was not. Lippincott declined to back the book. Burnett had to break the news that he would not be publishing the book after all. Salinger was livid. He couldn't see past the simple fact of his betrayal to the extenuating circumstances. He couldn't separate his champion, Burnett, from the people upstairs.

As Salinger's fame grew, Burnett, who was also struggling to keep his magazine financially afloat, reached out to Salinger on many occasions to lend his name to various projects, and was constantly rebuffed. When I brought this up to Burnett's son John, he described Salinger as having been "conveniently forgetful."

"He usually showed up for class late . . . and contrived to slip out early" is how Salinger recalled Burnett's teaching style. "I often have my doubts whether any good and conscientious short-story-course conductor can humanly do more. Except that Mr. Burnett did. I have several notions how or why he did, but it seems essential only to say that he had a passion for good short fiction . . ."

What comes across from both Mailer's and Salinger's renditions of Burnett is a sense of personal charisma. Half his accomplishment seems to have been to not particularly care that the kid in the back was smoking, looking out the window, and doing no work. At the time Burnett was separating from his wife and *Story* cofounder, Martha Foley, and was already involved with Hallie Southgate, with whom he would edit and publish *Story* for almost three more decades.

Foley, who would go on to edit the Best American Short Stories series for many years, wrote a memoir of the early days of *Story* that includes a striking image: Burnett had just arrived to work at the San Francisco newspaper where Foley was employed. He told her that he had traveled there by train and that he could only afford the ticket by working in exchange for the ride. His job was to ride standing in the cattle car and pick up the cows when they fell over. It had been a cross-country trip.

In November 1939, after nearly two whole semesters of dormancy, Salinger came to life. "He began to write," Burnett later wrote. "Several stories seemed to come from his typewriter at once . . ."

True to form, Salinger broke his silence not with a story but with a letter to Burnett. Salinger writes that he hadn't been fair to Burnett. He hadn't been doing the reading for class. He looks back at the nearly two semesters he spent in the back row of Burnett's class as though it were a concluded episode and characterizes them in the way someone with bad allergies might speak of a long nature walk in springtime. The symptoms weren't endless sneezing and itchy eyes, but they were just as debilitating. He refers to complexes and strange egos.

The word "ego" gets used often enough that I wondered, at first, if Salinger had read Freud, or if the college dropout two times over who was living at home had been to a psychoanalyst.[1]

---

1 The one bit of evidence suggesting this topic had been broached is the way John, in "A Girl I Knew," summarizes his activities in Vienna: "I spent a little

However it happened, Salinger had assimilated some of Freud's language, which he used to describe his afflictions in the past tense. It's a letter of expressive joy and optimism. He is free. And though he doesn't come out and say it, the letter gives every indication that his liberator is the person he is writing to, Whit Burnett.

Shortly after this letter, Salinger delivered several stories at once to Burnett.

One of them, "The Young Folks," impressed Burnett sufficiently that he suggested Salinger submit it to *Collier's* — one of the slicks that paid huge sums for contrived short stories with a twist at the end. It was a sly, almost passive-aggressive maneuver, and a win-win for the teacher/editor. If *Collier's* took the story, he would be proud of his student. If it didn't, he could consider the story for his magazine without bearing all the weight of his student's expectation.

Salinger was so jazzed by this development that he delivered the manuscript to *Collier's* in person. When it was rejected, he brought it to Burnett. Almost a month passed.

Then, on January 15, 1940, shortly after Salinger's twenty-first birthday, Burnett delivered the good news: "The Young Folks" would be Salinger's first publication.

Salinger wrote him back immediately in a state of elation tinged with panic. The letter begins by comparing himself to a pair of cold, damp hands. The image echoes the finger preoccupations of the story's protagonist, evokes the strangled atmosphere of Sherwood Anderson's story "Hands" in *Winesburg, Ohio,* and signals the start of a major literary motif in Salinger's work.

---

more than five months in Vienna. I danced. I went ice skating and skiing. For strenuous exercise, I argued with an Englishman. I watched operations at two hospitals and had myself psychoanalyzed by a young Hungarian woman who smoked cigars."

Salinger writes as though he has been summoned to an imaginary podium to receive an imaginary award. He delivers an acceptance speech of sorts. He is twenty-one, he writes Burnett, and can elicit a rejection slip with one hand tied behind his back. Now that a short story of his will see print he can refuse any further acts of self-pity. His ego — that word again — will be able to withstand whatever people and circumstances throw at him. He will no longer be his own worst enemy.

The recurring hand imagery, the repeated references to the ego, the anxiety that he is pitied, the concept of self-defeat — it's as though Salinger has woken from a dream to find himself in a reverse of Kafka's *The Metamorphosis,* turning from bug to man.[2]

Hallie Burnett, Whit's second wife, would later describe Salinger's gestational silence in the back of the room as a "purposeful reverie." But to me it sounds like a man waking from a paralysis to discover, in rapid succession, that he can walk, that he can run, that he can run fast.

Two weeks later, on January 28, 1940, Salinger writes Burnett again to report that he has been more or less doing a nonstop happy dance for two straight weeks, with breaks to allow for publicizing this epic news. The letter includes a list of imaginary reactions by friends and schoolmates upon being told the momentous news of his forthcoming debut. Even paraphrasing the list it's clear that each line is an ironic putdown:

- He's been going on about getting published for so long I can't believe it finally happened.

---

2 Kafka was a writer Salinger cited as a favorite, and he is a kind of amulet I carry with me through my explorations of Salinger's life. There is a lot of resonance between the two writers: the terrible relationship with their fathers, their intense connection to the landscape of their cities, the aura of allegory in their work, so strong in Kafka's but felt in Salinger's, too. Then there is Kafka's dying wish, expressed to his friend Max Brod, that his papers be burned.

- The guy failed out of two schools; it's impossible to imagine him doing anything.
- He's a Jew.
- If you have ever thought of going on a date with him, take it from me and don't.

The list is a fascinating amalgam of self-aggrandizement and self-loathing. In February Salinger writes to Burnett that he had planned to go away on a trip, but that his parents went away instead. So he stays home alone. He celebrates, drinks beer, and moves his typewriter from room to room—"magnesia white" feathers everywhere.

"The Young Folks" begins:

> About eleven o'clock, Lucille Henderson, observing that her party was soaring at the proper height, and just having been smiled at by Jack Delroy, forced herself to glance over in the direction of Edna Phillips, who since eight o'clock had been sitting in the big red chair, smoking cigarettes and yodeling hellos and wearing a very bright eye which young men were not bothering to catch. Edna's direction still the same, Lucille Henderson sighed as heavily as her dress would allow, and then, knitting what there was of her brows, gazed about the room at the noisy young people she had invited to drink up her father's Scotch. Then abruptly she swished to where William Jameson Junior sat, biting his fingernails and staring at a small blonde girl sitting on the floor with three young men from Rutgers.

Reading this is like discovering a photograph of a beloved person when she was very young. You can see in that child's face the grown-up she will eventually become, all of it already in a sense written on her face. Such moments are exciting in part because they make us feel powerful in our discovery, and they make us feel totally helpless, too, almost infantile, because there it all is, the map already drawn.

So much of the method and tone of Salinger's later work is already present. There is the sense of misdirection — we start focused on someone who is not the focus — and the mischievous bounce and rhyme of the line that goes along with it, as we boppity-bop our way toward the story's center, which is the sadness of a girl whose precarious resilience doesn't do all that much to make her sympathetic. We are left in the uncomfortable position of wondering if we should feel pity for William Jameson for his ineptness, or for Edna Phillips, for having her "bright eye" be so insistently unmet.

The story is no masterpiece, but it's alive in that mysterious Salinger way. He seems to have emerged fully formed and situated directly in the middle of his sweet spot, by which I mean the age for which he seems to have the most effortless empathy and whose music he hears most clearly — callow youth, that period in life when a kind of clueless self-absorption mixes with a genuine if spasmodically expressed generosity of spirit. In this story — his very first publication — there is also the brinksmanship present in so much of his later work, where Salinger seems to be pushing his characters to the edge of unlikability before redeeming them. I suspect this is why he has such an amazing ability to animate his characters by their relationship to their fingers, the gnawing of hangnails and fingernails and so on. There is something so absurd and comic about the preoccupation with one's own fingers, and yet so totally understandable, so forgivable.

The story ends with a small crime committed by Edna. Foreshadowing elisions in Salinger's subsequent work, it happens out of sight, offstage. We have to infer the act and wonder what it might mean.

"The Daring Young Man
on the Flying Trapeze"

Someone who isn't a writer begins to want to be a writer
and he keeps on wanting to be one for ten years, and by
that time he has convinced all his relatives and friends
and even himself that he *is* a writer, but he hasn't written a
thing and he is no longer a boy, so he is getting worried.

— WILLIAM SAROYAN, preface to the first edition,
The Daring Young Man on the Flying Trapeze, and Other Stories

EVEN THOUGH Salinger wrote to Burnett praising
William Saroyan's story "Seventy Thousand Assyrians," Saroyan should be of only passing interest in talking about J.D. Salinger. Yet there is a strong undercurrent in the
central epiphany of Saroyan's early stories that appears in Salinger's work as well — a kind of radical transparency in which narrator and author are practically indistinguishable. By today's
standards Saroyan's stories read like personal essays. Yet they are
also touched by the surreal.

Saroyan became famous in 1934 on the strength of one
rather short and strange story, "The Daring Young Man on the
Flying Trapeze," that Whit Burnett took for *Story* magazine.
A book of stories with the same title shortly followed. It was a
phenomenal success. He wrote plays, movies, even a hit song.

For about eight years Saroyan moved between the worlds of literature and show business with ease. He made a lot of money. He was praised by critics. He won a Pulitzer Prize for a play and had the confidence to turn it down.

"The Daring Young Man on the Flying Trapeze" is divided into two sections: a brief introductory one called "Sleep" and a longer one called "Wakefulness." "Sleep" comprises four surreal, dreamy sentences that seem to be both modernist and primitive. "Wakefulness" is only slightly more realistic in the way it's written: The protagonist is a starving writer who sets out on his day. Starving is not a euphemism here. A bit like Kafka's hungry artist, this man is starving to death. And, as in Kafka's story, at the end he dies.

It's tempting to say that such a morbid vision would appeal to an American public in the grip of the Great Depression, but that probably misses the point of Saroyan's appeal, or only touches on part of it. Saroyan's great talent was to infuse a warmth and bonhomie into his material that would otherwise seem dark — thus a feel-good, starving-to-death story. His voice was unashamedly philosophical, proudly rudimentary and unpolished. The quality of being unembarrassed may have been Saroyan's gift and curse. James Agee called him "a gifted Schmaltz artist."

"Seventy Thousand Assyrians" is a report on the lamentations of an Assyrian man who is cutting the narrator's hair. From Saroyan, Salinger may have learned something about the value of a small setting and how it can resonate far beyond the walls of the room in which the story takes place. He might have been impressed by the expansive confidence of Saroyan's narrating voice — see the remarkable gusto of Salinger's opening lines, especially the stories in the third person ("There were ninety-seven New York advertising men in the hotel ..."). But most of all he may have been intrigued by the gamesmanship in the stories, the way Saroyan keeps breaking the fourth wall to address his readers — a hustler distracting his audience with the apparent simplicity of his tale while effecting a subtle change in them.

Saroyan's fame didn't last; it vanished almost as fast as it appeared. He would later blame this on the war and two bad marriages to the same woman, Carol Marcus, who happened to be best friends with a woman who would mean a lot to Salinger, Oona O'Neill.

Once you start staring at someone's life certain resonances appear, and there are a number of them with Saroyan and Salinger. A minor one is the professionalism with which they approached their craft, with an emphasis on productivity, and the fact that each had a nearly spiritual relationship to his typewriter. Less minor is their relationships with their fathers. Salinger had a bad relationship with his father; Saroyan lost his father when he was three. Yet another echo is the complicated way that both of these men would be written about by their children. William Saroyan's first biographer was Aram Saroyan, his son. Aram writes of his father being left at an orphanage at the age of three by his mother, who admonishes the sobbing boy. He speculates that being told not to cry, as opposed to being comforted, froze something deep within his father. He writes it in a dispassionate way, though; it reminds me, slightly, of the way Margaret Salinger's book swerves between autobiography and biography, with the latter being quite dispassionate in tone. Finally, there is an observation about Saroyan by the critic Nona Balakian, which also resonates with Salinger, about the relationship between the author's life and work: "Taking a cue from the writer himself, we allowed the man to take precedence over the work."

23

1133 Park Avenue

THE AWNING IS GREEN, and located off Park Avenue on Ninety-First Street. It is a warm spring day, the air filled with light drizzle. The tulips on Park Avenue are completely open, faltering but still glorious. The lobby is a tiny box; I come through the front doors and could have reached the elevator in ten steps. The doorman calls my name upstairs. Then I am in a tiny elevator, real wood paneling, art deco in design, rattling upward.

I had made getting into the Salinger apartment a kind of holy grail. I had written to almost everyone I knew and many people I didn't. At one point I thought I'd found a contact to let me in, but then that person suddenly became vague. She was busy. Her kid was touring colleges, I was told. I waited a month and wrote again. "It's not going to work, I am sorry" was the reply.

Was it guilt? More than once, when I told people I was working on a Salinger biography, they said, only half joking, "Leave that man alone!"

But I found another contact and now I was due for a tour of the building.

Prewar New York City apartments are central to J.D. Salinger's sensibility and to his work. An apartment can become, especially in those instances in which the residents have an instinct for holding on to things, a kind of physical manifestation of the mind that moves within its walls. Seeing his apartment was an attempt to walk the map of the author's consciousness. And, of course, I wanted to see if I would recognize it from his stories.

The tour was necessary because I still did not know in which apartment, exactly, the Salingers had lived. But there were only two apartments per floor. I could get a close enough idea. What was unclear to me, as I rattled upward in the elevator, was whether I was excited about seeing the place where the Salinger family had lived, or if I was excited about seeing the place where the Glass family had lived. Or the Caulfields. Or where Ginnie had sat waiting for Selena to come out of the bedroom with the taxi money in "Just Before the War with the Eskimos."

What I knew for a fact was that the Salingers had moved here in 1932 and that Sol and Miriam lived here for almost four decades. I knew that Doris Salinger had been married in this apartment in 1935, and that the marriage didn't last. I knew that this was the apartment where J.D. Salinger must have first conceived and written almost all the characters for which he is famous, and the apartment to which he had brought his first wife when he finally returned home from Europe after the war. But what was foremost on my mind was not biography but fiction.

The day before I had been down to Princeton to read "The Last and Best of the Peter Pans." Written in 1942, it shares with most of the stories written in these first years a tremendous sense of anxiety about the coming war, seen not so much from the point of view of the men who are going to fight it, but of their mothers. That is the tension, and subject, at the heart of "The Last and Best of the Peter Pans."

The story begins: "My mother is . . ." and goes on to explain that she is not just an actress, but *the* actress; a star of stage and screen.

The story, told by Vincent Caulfield, begins with a long, rhapsodic monologue about the mother in a voice very simi-

lar to Holden Caulfield's at the start of *The Catcher in the Rye*.
Things get a little bizarre when the narrator describes his mother's portrayal of Juliet in *Romeo and Juliet*. The narrator's father,
by the way, is also an actor, and is playing Romeo. His performance is alluded to and dismissed as "tightsy," a word that gave
me pause. A Salingerian invention. Meaning, I decided, given
the play, "a person conspicuously wearing tights." Actory. Artificial. Not quite venomous enough to imply "phony," but in the
vicinity. The mother's acting, meanwhile, is on another plane.
Of her performance, we are told, "mother wrought on the Cap-
ulets all the sad, vicious wiles of a truthful kid turned liar."

Even though the narrator, Vincent, was a young boy when
he saw this performance, he instinctively knows that he is
watching a young girl in love. Which is also an arresting comment, as his mother was, at the time of this Juliet performance,
thirty-eight years old.

All this is prelude to the story's central conflict, which
would never have occurred if the family did not have a new
maid who was in the habit of delivering the narrator's breakfast,
a soft-boiled egg, in an egg cup with no spoon.[1] A few days of
having to ask for a spoon go by until, in exasperation, the narrator heads to the pantry himself to get his own spoon.

The previous day I had imbibed this fleeting passage — maid
brings breakfast; no spoon; guy goes to kitchen to get
one — without really thinking the whole thing through. How
many steps would this take? The story's central plot point is
what he finds in the pantry, nestled among the spoons: a letter
from the army, of not recent vintage, which his mother had hid-

---

1 For some reason this makes me think of a scandal that would have swept
over the Salinger household in 1941, when J.S. Hoffman and Co. was convicted
of the crime of distributing fake Swiss cheese. The company had been boring
holes in cheese from Wisconsin. The Salinger fortune survived, but it was reported in the *New York Times*.

den from him.[2] Soon we are at the heart of the matter, which is a long extended confrontation between mother and son in her bedroom.

After discovering the induction notice the narrator takes the shortest possible route from the kitchen to where his mother sits in her bedroom, which was "through the dining room wall." He speaks to her "calmly and intelligently."

She replies (being an actor she gets the good lines): "Stop shouting."

We are about six pages into the story at this point. The remaining six pages consist mostly of dialogue.

The story is deeply great. I couldn't think of why Salinger had refrained from publishing it, or put such draconian restrictions on it, forbidding its publication until after his death.

Then I thought of "Go See Eddie," a story written a year before "The Last and Best of the Peter Pans," around the same time as "The Young Folks." The story concerns a grown-up brother and sister exchanging threats and sparring over a cup of coffee in her room, where she has just thrown on a robe. Here, sex isn't a subtext — the Eddie of the title is a lecherous producer to whom the brother wants to pimp his sister in order to settle a debt. When she resists he threatens to out her affair with a married man. At the end we discover her capacity for sexual deceit goes beyond anything her brother imagined.

"Go See Eddie" is a fascinating counterpoint to "The Last and Best of the Peter Pans." The two stories are completely different in tone and substance, and yet their staging makes them

2 The spoon omission can be read as a commentary on either the maid's ineptness or her guile; it's possible the prince of the house was a sufficient jerk that the new maid had already declared a war of subterfuge. Or perhaps the war was on the queen of the house. Knowing what was amid the spoons, her delivering a soft-boiled egg with no spoon is cunning.

seem to be each other's doppelgänger: Both unfold almost entirely in a room whose center of gravity is a woman sitting at a dressing table. Both contain a scene in which a woman is confronted with an angry, aggressive man. In "Go See Eddie" the man is her brother. In "The Last and Best of the Peter Pans" it's her son. Much is made of the beauty of both women. They are both actresses — the sister is at the bottom of the show biz totem pole or near to it; the mother is not just an actress but a star. Both are in robes. Both have voluptuous red hair that they spend a lot of time combing, a nearly defensive gesture given the men staring at them. Both women are deceptive. But "The Last and Best of the Peter Pans" has the innovation of that gentle, fumbling voice — exasperated, dire, and jokey all at once — that presages so much of Salinger's later work. It has Vincent Caulfield at its center (Holden is alluded to). It has a gorgeous moment when the mother spots Phoebe Caulfield down on the sidewalk and notes her lovely dress.

The elevator door opened. My host stood in the doorway of her apartment. I walked forward thinking that I was now going to see the kitchen, and wondered how many steps it was to the bedroom, the bedroom where, perhaps, some model of that dressing table might have sat.

Instead I took one step forward, glanced to my right, and saw a hallway, at the far side of which was the open door of a bathroom and the gleaming white bathtub in which Zooey Glass had sat with letter in hand and cigarette smoldering.

I saw several apartments that day. Later I would discover the exact Salinger apartment and visit. It's on the west line, three bedrooms, two maids' rooms to the east line's one. The apartments, today, use the maids' rooms as offices or small bedrooms. In Salinger's youth, I was told, they were mostly occupied by live-in maids.

I discovered that the man living directly below the Salinger apartment is a psychiatrist who treated Kurt Vonnegut; he
is mentioned by name in a collection of Vonnegut's letters, and
goes and gets the recently published book to read the passage to
me out loud. At first this seems pretty random, but it later occurs to me that Vonnegut was also a veteran of the Battle of the
Bulge.

Perhaps the most notable feature of the whole apartment is
the view, which, though only on the sixth floor, is unusually expansive because diagonally across Park Avenue is the Brick Pres-
byterian Church and its elegant white spire. Also a clock. Not
quite as big as something Harold Lloyd would hang from, but
an interesting feature in the view from your childhood apartment, I should think.

There was a strange serendipity that day: I was standing in the
living room with my back to the kitchen door, calculating that,
yes, the shortest route from the kitchen to the bedroom would
be to walk through that wall, when my host handed me an article on the front page of the *Times* arts section featuring a photograph of J.D. Salinger. I had come here to commune with Salinger and now here he was, but with the complication that a
million other people were also communing with him. For those
among the vast *Times* readership who are Salinger fans, a decent
number in all likelihood, this would trigger a curious compart-
mentalization, not unlike what teenagers do with pop stars and
lots and lots of people do with God — his presence there in the
paper was just an outward manifestation of a voice whose real
presence and meaning were directed, in some way, at them. This
is part of the Salinger genius — even when his audience became,
at least for a while, enormous, the work spoke directly to each
individual.

The photo was taken in 1952, a year after *The Catcher in*

the Rye was published. Salinger's gaze is directed off to the side, handsome, confident, but soulful and a bit devilish. The photographer was named Antony di Gesu. Salinger had commissioned it. He said he wanted to have a photograph of himself to give to his mother.

24

1941: "A Young Girl in 1941 with No Waist at All"

IN EARLY 1941 Salinger took a job on the cruise ship *Kungsholm,* bound for a nineteen-day trip to the Caribbean. He took the job alongside his friend Herb Kauffman, with whom he had once gone door-to-door in New York looking for acting work.

He would later write half jokingly about having a drawer full of cruise stories. The only one that made it into a book was "Teddy." The other that saw publication was "A Young Girl in 1941 with No Waist at All," which appeared in *Mademoiselle* in 1947. It is a companion story to "A Girl I Knew." Both were written in 1946–47, at a time when Salinger was trying to get his bearings in the wake of returning from the war. Both are imbued with a fascinating subtext of a writer reaching back across an experience to a life that now must seem remote, but that he needs to feel near. And both foreshadow the coming war.

The basis for "A Young Girl in 1941 with No Waist at All" is autobiographical, though Salinger fudges details. He was a big adjuster of minor details, moving his dates and streets slightly away from their real-life moorings to allow them to further drift into imaginative life. In the case of this story it is set in 1940, though he was on the SS *Kungsholm* in 1941.

The story bears striking similarities to some biographical

details of Salinger's life: its male lead, Ray Kinsella, is on the staff of a cruise ship that is docked outside Havana. Like a salsa dance step that starts on an offbeat, Salinger reserves the deliciously meandering and fluid opening line with which he had begun so many of his early stories for the second line. The first is relatively straightforward, a rare moment when the syntactical rhythm is more Hemingway than Fitzgerald: "The young man in the seat behind Barbara at the jai alai games had leaned forward finally and asked if she were ill and if she would like to be escorted back to the ship."

That "finally" makes all the difference, implying a long period of the guy wondering if he should say something because, one presumes, the young lady was somehow suffering noticeably. The next line, however, is the whole Salinger orchestra: "Barbara had looked up at him, had looked at his looks, and said yes, she thought she would, thank you, that she did have kind of a headache, and that it was certainly awfully nice of him."

If I were to choose one story from the first panel of the Salinger triptych to include in *Nine Stories* it would probably be this one, not so much for its overall effect as for the many tiny pleasures strewn throughout and the nearly surreal portrait of a married couple at its center, which may shed light on Salinger's own parents.

The small pleasures:

- The name for the small boat that ferries passengers from the ship to the dock and back: a "tender."
- A long make-out scene on the deck of a ship in which Ray is in a painfully awkward position, which he nevertheless holds for hours, sacrificing his body for the pleasures of Barbara's mouth.
- A lengthy scene in a Havana nightclub, in which we feel the louche, corrupt, mobbed-up glamor of Havana before its fall.

Mostly, though, I am transfixed by the middle-aged couple who take up the center of the story, attaching themselves to Ray and Barbara: Diane and Fielding Woodruff.

They are among the most peculiar characters Salinger ever rendered, right up there with the little man in a top hat who sits in the taxi in "Raise High the Roof Beam, Carpenters," except that unlike that man, who exists in the story as though transposed from the era of silent movies, Diane Woodruff cannot shut up. An attractive gray-haired woman with a pear-shaped diamond ring and a diamond bracelet, and "a long sleeved evening gown with Thurber dogs in the pattern," she is riveting, in part because her conversational patter strains toward cheerfulness with such vigor you expect her to collapse at any moment in despair. Her conversational style is to fire off a volley of instructions masquerading as questions:

"Isn't it a heavenly night?"
"Don't you just feel wonderful?"
"Fielding, darling, you look like a college boy, so young. It's indecent."
"We're from San Francisco. Isn't it wonderful? Do you think we'll be in the war soon, Mr. Walters? My husband doesn't think so."

Ray is going to be joining with an artillery commission from ROTC and is cheerful about it because he feels he will not have to take anyone's "guff," which is surely a send-up of Salinger's pre-army attitude, as he ended up taking a huge amount of guff along with everyone else and hating it.

I can't entirely resist finding in Salinger's portrait of the Woodruffs clues about his own parents. I don't think Salinger's mother, Miriam, was a ridiculous and drunken mess like Diane Woodruff. Nor do I think that Sol was quite so silent and drunk, to the point of being infantile, as Fielding. Nevertheless,

Miriam Salinger, probably like every other mother of a young son in 1941, was very wound up and upset about the prospect of her son going to war.

This is the chief concern for Diane Woodruff, too. After a period of dancing and carousing, Diane proclaiming on the joyousness of it all, she gets up to go to the bathroom. As soon as she leaves the table, her husband, suddenly alert,[1] announces that their son is enlisting in the army just then, back in San Francisco, unbeknownst to his mother.

Ray and Barbara eventually get into a tender and wind up on the ship's deck, making out. The scene is an occasion for Salinger to display his astonishing capacity to make tiny physical gestures seem both incredibly real and also confusing, a form of hyper-accuracy that should repel interest but instead does the opposite.

In between sessions of kissing there is conversation, and we discover that Barbara is engaged to be married, and that Ray is trying to convince her to ditch her fiancé and marry him instead. Her problem with this, at least the one she articulates, is that she wouldn't know what to tell her future mother-in-law, with whom she is traveling on the cruise. What she says after this is striking. She asks him, while biting "nervously at the cuticle of her thumb," if he thinks she is dumb.

> "Do I what? Do I think you're dumb? I certainly don't!"
> "I'm considered dumb," said Barbara slowly. "I am a little dumb. I guess."

---

1 If I had to name one thing that Salinger picked up from the Marx Brothers, it was an awareness of the comedic value of abruptness. Among the short stories Salinger published in magazines but did not collect into a book, the word "abruptly" is used exactly twenty times. "Exactly" is another favorite. But I am not going to count. Some things should remain mysterious.

"Now stop that talk. I mean, stop it. You're not dumb. You're smart. Who said you're dumb? That guy Carl?"

Barbara was vague about it. "Oh, not exactly. Girls, more. Girls I went to school with and go around with."

"They're crazy."

Neither Ray nor the reader fully recovers from the possibility that she is dumb. It is an example of a very strange theme in these early stories: the theme of the dumb girl. The story ends in her room, which she shares with her mother-in-law-to-be, who receives the news that her future daughter-in-law is going to back out of the marriage to her son with remarkable equanimity. It's a testimony to the story that the reader wonders if the mother-in-law is secretly delighted.

But the essential fascination of the story is the Woodruffs — embroiled, compressed, repressed, sexual, stunted, over-privileged, underprivileged, and profoundly perverse. Am I simply overreacting to the spectacle of a drunken middle-aged couple? Perhaps. But summon *Who's Afraid of Virginia Woolf?* and then think about this scene: When the tender bearing the party of four returns to the boat, the drunken middle-aged couple climb the flimsy ladder up to the ship. It's the first we've really heard of this ladder. Diane goes first.

At the top she shouts down at her husband, who is halfway up the ladder when she accuses him of holding the ladder while she climbed. He denies it. And then he sits down on the ladder and sulks. She climbs down to meet him on the ladder, briefly appears to strangle him, and then relaxes her hold.

"Do you love me, mouse?" she asked, practically cutting off his respiration. His reply was unintelligible. "Too tight?" asked Mrs. Woodruff. She relaxed her hold, looked out over the shimmering water and answered her own question. "Of course you love me. It would be unforgivable of you not to love me. Sweet boy, please don't fall; put both feet on the rung. How did you get so tight dear? I wonder why our marriage has been such a joy. We're so stinking rich. We should have, by all the rules, drifted continents apart. You do love me so much it's almost unbearable, don't you? Sweet, put both feet on the rung, like a good boy. Isn't it nice here?"

My notion that there is something significant about this couple that might reflect on Salinger's parents is informed by an anecdote about Sol and Miriam Salinger on a vacation cruise that I heard at the same time I was reading and rereading this story: In 1960, a young married couple who had just moved into 1133 Park Avenue took a cruise, and were amazed to see on the passenger list the name of another couple from their new building, Sol and Miriam Salinger. Shortly thereafter they go up to Sol and Miriam and introduce themselves as fellow shareholders at 1133. They spend some time together and seem to be friends. But a few days later the Salingers tell their new friends and neighbors that they are "much too young" and they needed to find people more their age. And that was that. It's quite possible the Salingers found this couple annoying; I don't doubt their motives but find significance in the abruptness of their style.

Women in Letters

J ERRY SALINGER MET Oona O'Neill in the summer of
1941 when Elizabeth Murray brought Salinger over to her
friend and neighbor Agnes O'Neill's house. Oona was fifteen, and already gossip column fodder along with her two close
friends Gloria Vanderbilt and Carol Marcus, the future wife of
William Saroyan (twice) and Walter Matthau, and the model
for Holly Golightly.

You can find plenty of photographs of Oona online, and
even a screen test from when she was still a teenager, but Salinger was a connoisseur of skin tone, of a certain glow, and I have a
feeling none of this photographic evidence conveys her effect in
person.[1] Her father was the famous playwright Eugene O'Neill.
But she had hardly seen him at all since he left her mother, Agnes, when Oona was two years old.

Oona and Jerry started going on dates in New York, par-
ticipating in the club scene of the day. The Stork Club wanted
to make a big splash announcing Oona as the debutante of the
year — she was turning sixteen — and Salinger pleaded with her
to forgo the whole thing. Salinger, like Holden, was such a connoisseur of phonies because he hung out with so many of them.

---

1 The novelist James Salter, who, like Oona, was born in 1925, reports: "I did
see Oona once or twice on the cross-town bus, and had to keep dropping my
eyes to overcome the absolute need to look at her."

Was Oona the love of his life? Or an epic crush and the object of his most intense ardor and lust? Or an occasion for social climbing? Or a trophy? I vote all of the above. Did he want to marry her and live with her forever? Maybe, but first he had to figure out a way to spend time with her unaccompanied by her mother.

His letter to Murray on September 15, 1941, begins with a lament about Agnes, who accompanied her daughter on all their dates.

However exasperated, he also sounds amused. Then the letter descends to a bitter note, calling Oona "spoiled." But then it lightens up again, saying at least it means people have been paying attention to Oona. Salinger abruptly turns his attention to the news that he has sent his latest story, "The Long Debut of Lois Taggett"—a story into which, he wrote Murray, he had deposited several quarts of his own blood—to his agent.

"The Long Debut of Lois Taggett" is about a society girl. At first, the author treats her with mere contempt:

Come springtime again and air-conditioning at the Stork Club, Lois fell in love. He was a tall press agent named Bill Tedderton, with a deep, dirty voice. He certainly wasn't anything to bring home to Mr. and Mrs. Taggett, but Lois figured he certainly was something to bring home. She fell hard, and Bill, who had been around plenty since he'd left Kansas City, trained himself to look deep into Lois' eyes to see the door to the family vault. Lois became Mrs. Tedderton, and the Taggetts didn't do very much about it. It wasn't fashionable any longer to make a row if your daughter preferred the iceman to that nice Astorbilt boy. Everybody knew, of course, that press agents were icemen. Same thing.

Then contempt turns into cruelty. Bill marries Lois for money but, in what at first seems like a happy twist, he falls in love with

her. The story is briefly cheerful. One day Bill reaches for his
cigarette and holds it like a pencil directly over her hand.

"Better not," said Lois, with mock warning. "Burny, burny."
But Bill, as though he hadn't heard, deliberately, yet almost
idly, did what he had to do.
Lois screamed horribly, wrenched herself to her feet, and ran
crazily out of the room.
Bill pounded on the bathroom door. Lois had locked it.
"Lois. Lois, baby. Darling. Honest to God. I didn't know
what I was doing. Lois. Darling. Open the door."

For a moment the reader wonders if this is a story about crazy
love. It's not. This is the beginning of the torment of Lois
Taggett, which increases to a pitch of sadism.

Knowing the story was written in such proximity to his dat-
ing Oona is chilling. My most generous assessment is that this
is the anguish, and rage, a guy feels when he is besotted with a
beautiful woman who is already slipping away even when she
is in your arms. The events of the story are bad enough; but as
usual with Salinger, it's the tone that conveys the most power.

Ian Hamilton describes Lois at the end of the story, when
events have beaten all the glamor and hope out of her, as having
been "becalmed." His exact phrase: "Thus Lois is becalmed: she
is neither grand nor phony."

I found Hamilton's use of this word provocative in its Nurse
Ratched–like serenity. In this context, "becalmed" has echoes of
castration, lobotomy, a violent quelling. Not what one expects
from a champion of authenticity.[2]

---

2 "Elaine," written a year or so later, is even more conspicuously violent in
its attitude toward the main female character who, like Barbara in "A Young
Girl in 1941 with No Waist at All," is pretty and dumb. Elaine is both pret-
tier and dumber. She likes to go to the movies and lives with her mother in

In addition to the pants-down obviousness of the association between Oona and Lois in the story, there is also an element of the uncanny in Salinger's reference to "the iceman."

Eugene O'Neill's play *The Iceman Cometh* had been written in 1939, but it would not be performed until several years after Salinger wrote the story. Maybe Salinger heard it discussed. Maybe the whole story was a twisted letter to Oona. Or maybe it qualifies as a psychic moment. According to O'Neill's biographer Arthur Gelb, O'Neill kept the title *Long Day's Journey into Night*, written at around the same time, top secret, but *The Iceman Cometh* was a title in circulation. Oona must certainly have heard it and mentioned it for Salinger to make such a direct allusion, which is to say I am betting on gossip and chatter trumping psychic powers.

Salinger didn't take the end of the Oona affair well, in part because it didn't seem to have a distinct end. His rage was surely compounded by a sense of helplessness — he was now stationed in Bainbridge, Georgia. He had been about a week away from seeing his first story in *The New Yorker* when Pearl Harbor was

---

the Bronx. We meet her at age six shortly after her father has dropped dead, and follow her into her teen years in a series of brief vignettes whose primary purpose is to reaffirm her beauty and her dumbness. Really, she is on the borderline of disabled, it would seem. And very beautiful. When she is sixteen Salinger allows her to be coerced by a young man to join him for a day at the beach, and then on a walk under the boardwalk. To say that he "allows" her is a strange way to put it, but then Salinger would always insist on his characters' autonomy, which in turn allowed him to dote on them with a parental kind of love. The last we hear of this walk on the beach is from the point of view of Elaine's date, when he has maneuvered Elaine to a remote spot under the boardwalk: "His mediocre heart had begun to pound excitedly, because with the eternal rake's despicable but seldom faulty intuition, he knew it was going to be easy . . . so easy . . ." The boy's name is Teddy.

Perhaps Salinger has a specific motive in wanting to suppress these early stories, with their strange hostility toward women.

bombed. Oona, who was in Hollywood, had been receiving letters almost daily from Salinger. She thought they were warm and witty, though their charm was undoubtedly undercut by their frequency.

The relationship was over. But it wasn't. Which is to say that if you are in the position of the besotted Jerry Salinger, stuck on an army base in Georgia while your girl is in Hollywood trying to break into the movies, it's still not over until it is really and irrefutably over — which is when you have been replaced.

The loathed replacement is an iconic figure. A lot of obsessive energy has gone into hating the replacement. What would it be like if the replacement was a famous actor, one of the most beloved and recognizable characters in the world?

In November, Salinger writes to Murray in a stressed mood. His typed letters are remarkably free from spelling errors or even mistyped or blacked-out words or letters; he's a very fastidious typist. It's impressive. But this one has an uncharacteristic splotch of Xs over a word. He regales her with his professional news. Houghton Mifflin has written to him, he says, encouraging him to apply for its next fellowship contest. But, he quips, it failed to arrange an end to the war.[3]

He mentions the now lost story, "The Kissless Life of Reilly" (which sounds as if it might involve a lovelorn soldier stuck on an army base), and claims it was born out of his ruminations about the difference between suicide and murdering yourself. He doubts that editors will go for it, a feeling that would turn out to be correct.

The letter ends with his blurting out that he would marry Oona without hesitation if only she would agree to marry him,

---

3 Did he do this with his mother? I would guess not. The intensity of her gaze was too overwhelming. And she was too far removed from the world of literary life, to which Murray had more access intellectually and socially.

and fantasizes of taking all his money from the *Collier's* sale and going out to Hollywood to propose.

Six months later, on June 11, he writes Murray with snide, defensive jokes about Oona leaving her undergarments lying around Charlie Chaplin's apartment. He professes to find the whole idea of Oona rather distant and abstract — he's over it, in other words — but then adds that he would like to give Agnes a kick in the ass and calls Chaplin an old prostate gland.

The effort to appear above it all is a strain but his effort is admirable. About six weeks later, on July 19, he writes a letter whose cool is much diminished. You can hear the visceral disgust of the rejected lover as he imagines how the couple's domestic bliss would play out in the bedroom. He characterizes a part of Chaplin's anatomy as a dead rat. It's a hateful outburst, and in the end he collapses into apology and remorse for saying those things.

The feeling of portent around Salinger's letters to both Burnett and Murray, from the point of view of someone reading (or writing) a biography after Salinger's death, is so strong — the knowledge that these letters would be the foundation of Ian Hamilton's biography and the cause of Salinger's lawsuit, an operatic crescendo to the strange drama of his gathering in of all the words he had once so eagerly sent out, including his early stories — that it's hard to read them as letters. They seem like literary documents that belong in a book.

Oona had been in Los Angeles spending time with Carol Marcus, who was feverishly corresponding with her newly enlisted husband, William Saroyan. He wrote her every day. He had instructed her to write him back daily. Carol was flustered by the deadlines, and Oona casually remarked that she was getting besieged by letters from Jerry Salinger, and they had some good parts. Why didn't Carol use them?

Thus Jerry Salinger became a kind of Cyrano de Bergerac

on behalf of Carol Marcus, who copied out parts of his letters and mailed them off to her husband under her own name. The punch line — and it is absurdly neat — to the purloined letters drama takes place a decade later on Charlie Chaplin's yacht, where the Chaplins and the Saroyans are having a nice time. Saroyan comes out of his cabin waving a copy of *The Catcher in the Rye* and raving on about how this Salinger kid could really write. Carol and Oona tell all. There is laughter and the sound of ice cubes clinking in glasses.

26

The Fan

I N SEPTEMBER 1941 a young woman from Toronto
named Marjorie Sheard wrote to Salinger asking for advice
about getting published.

Sheard was about his age and had read his stories "The Hang
of It" and "The Heart of a Broken Story" in *Collier's* and *Esquire,* respectively. At the start of that year he had written mo-
rosely to Elizabeth Murray about the soggy cornflakeness of his
life. In the interval he had published those stories.

He had gone, in less than eighteen months, from staring va-
cantly out the window at the back of Whit Burnett's University
Extension class to getting fan letters. And in spite of the large
sums that these magazines paid, the address from which he was
writing remained 1133 Park Avenue.

Salinger's reply was the start of a correspondence that would
total nine letters from him. He is courteous, flattering to his
flatterer, and writes with the barely contained excitement of a
kid emerging onto the ice in skates he barely knows how to use,
his tone full of scampering energy and excitement. Now and
then the arms go flying out for balance but Salinger, an expert
dancer, never really falls, except once — having been so courteous and encouraging he suddenly writes a curt note command-
ing her to send him her picture. This abrupt shift feels like a guy
on a date for whom the pretense of decorum has become too

exhausting to maintain, so he drops it and lunges at his companion.

But this is immediately followed up with another note to Sheard in which he is contrite and apologizes for his ugly mood.

Unless Salinger slaved over his letters, typing multiple drafts, what jumps out at you is the neatness of the page and the typing. Not one typo. And the fluidity of the warmth that flows from the lines. The mixture of the informal and the profound, even in this artificial exchange of writing to a fan, is remarkable.

The correspondence is the first appearance of a major theme: Salinger writing to a young woman with advice and encouragement, with a nod to the edge of the map where there be dragons, and Vassar girls. The practical advice he offers — avoid Ivy League phoniness at all costs, let the honest instincts prevail — is quite similar to the advice he would dispense, usually to women, for the rest of his life.

He suggests she try sending her work to small magazines such as *Decade,* the *Kansas City University Review,* and *Mademoiselle.* If you can't get much money from the small magazines, it doesn't really matter, he says, implying that literary glory is what counts. But of course money did matter, as he well knew. He was never naive or overly romantic about this in his own affairs. Although he could comfortably live at his parents' apartment, his parents' apartment was the only place he could live, comfortably or otherwise, based on the $25 he was paid by *Story.* And he had to politely bother Burnett to get it.

To follow your instincts as a writer, to avoid pandering, to not care about anything other than your art — this was all excellent, timeless advice. You can't fault him for giving it, even if he wasn't following it himself. The story Sheard had read in *Collier's,* "The Hang of It," was a contrived army parable about which he had no illusions — he had told Elizabeth Murray to skip it. Many of his early, army-based stories were written as a means to get his name into the slicks.

The ebb and flow of their correspondence is marked by the request for a photo. It's a dustup of his own creation. The intensity and nature of his contrition is interesting for the way that he seems to be almost begging her forgiveness, wishing that she not turn her attention away. This is not politeness. This is genuine need.

Boorish or awkward behavior that is redeemed by self-awareness, or self-mockery, is a Salinger theme in both art and life. I want to say it is a sign of his artistry that it is more appealing in the art. But it was appealing enough in life. Sheard sends him a picture. He writes back that she is pretty, promises to send one of himself though he is out right now, having sent his last one to a little magazine. It sounds fishy. His compliment about her looks, and all his encouraging words to her, are perched on the precarious and rather fascinating edge between an almost paternal form of supportiveness and flirtation.

In one of the letters Salinger tells Sheard to look out for a story in *The New Yorker*. It was set to run in the first week of December 1941. Written in the third person, it featured a character named Holden Caulfield. When Pearl Harbor was attacked, the magazine decided to pull the story. I don't know exactly how fast this decision was made and conveyed to the author, but on December 11, 1941, probably a couple of days after getting the news, Salinger wrote to William Maxwell at *The New Yorker* saying that he had a second story about Holden but was going to hold on to it. He is pretty sure he is not going to do a series on him, he says, but, with the suavity of a guy opening a trench coat to display rows of watches for sale, he goes on to tell him about a story he is going to send about a fat prep school kid and his two blundering sisters.

27

The Lady Upstairs

CERTAIN VOICES take you back to places you have never been. That was what happened the first time I heard Kenny Karlstein talking about J.D. Salinger's sister, Doris. By the time he arrived at Bloomingdale's in 1968, Doris Salinger's career had peaked and was in eclipse.

"She was from another era," he said. "They used to go to the European collections on the *Queen Mary*! At one point she had been the fashion director at Bloomingdale's. After that she bought for the Green Room."

"You mean the part of the store that sold couture?" I asked.

"There is no couture in this country," he said, exasperated. The Green Room was where the store featured the top designers of the day. When Doris was moved out of that job, in the late 1960s, she took over a department that sold large sizes, where, Kenny said, "she had fantastic numbers."

It was Kenny's idea to go visit the satellite stores and not just concentrate on the main Fifty-Ninth Street store. And Doris, looking for new horizons at this stage of her career, asked if she could go with him. Once a week, on Thursday, they would drive out to Short Hills, New Jersey, among other places — a kind of *Driving Miss Daisy* of retail.

And during these long chatty drives, did she ever talk about her brother? I wondered.

"She was a sophisticated woman. She understood her

brother very well. She would talk about a niece. She never complained about him. Never!"

And what about his work?

"She told me her brother wrote about her. '*Franny and Zooey*,' she said, 'that was us.'"

While working on my biography of Salinger I had been interested in his real-life sister in part because his fictional sisters are among his most vivid and sympathetically drawn characters. But was Doris a model for them? In *The Catcher in the Rye* Holden Caulfield's sister, Phoebe, is astonishingly endearing and vivid. The scene where she shows up to meet Holden dragging along a suitcase of hers so she can join him on his journey is one of Salinger's most memorable.

And then there is Franny Glass of *Franny and Zooey,* exceptionally attractive, mysteriously bereft. The aura of style around Franny as a character extends to the book itself, whose design Salinger oversaw, going so far as to reject seventeen different shades of white for the cover before Little, Brown, his publisher, sent him a white he found suitable. (It was plain white house paint, which he had asked for all along.)

Franny's charisma, and the role of clothes in Salinger's depiction of it, can be summed up in the line describing her boyfriend seeing her on a train platform.

> Franny was among the first of the girls to get off the train . . . Lane spotted her immediately, and despite whatever it was he was trying to do with his face, his arm that shot up into the air was the whole truth. Franny saw it, and him, and waved extravagantly back. She was wearing a sheared raccoon coat, and Lane, walking toward her quickly . . . , reasoned to himself, with suppressed excitement, that he was the only one on the platform who really *knew* Franny's coat. He remembered that once . . . after kissing Franny for a half an hour or so, he had kissed her coat lapel, as

though it were a perfectly desirable, organic extension of the person herself.

Textures, fabrics, patterns: I can think of few writers as attuned to the role of clothes and fabric and design in the lives of their characters as J.D. Salinger. Here is the opening to one of his earliest stories, featuring Holden Caulfield ten years before the publication of *The Catcher in the Rye:*

> On vacation from Pencey Preparatory School for Boys ("An Instructor for Every Ten Students"), Holden Morrisey Caulfield usually wore his chesterfield and a hat with a cutting edge at the "V" in the crown. While riding on Fifth Avenue buses, girls who knew Holden often thought they saw him walking past Saks' or Altman's or Lord & Taylor's, but it was usually somebody else.

We then meet Holden's opposite number, Sally Hayes, also on vacation from her prep school, in the next deliberately repetitive paragraph:

> On vacation from Mary A. Woodruff, Sally usually went hatless and wore her new silverblu muskrat coat. While riding in Fifth Avenue buses, boys who knew Sally often thought they saw her walking past Saks' or Altman's or Lord & Taylor's. It was usually somebody else.

Salinger writes of the department stores of New York in the same offhanded way he writes about the other landmarks of the city: Grand Central Station, the American Museum of Natural History, Central Park — they are not monuments to be ogled; they are part of the landscape through which his characters move. That his older sister worked at Bloomingdale's made sense.

Salinger was a poet of clothing and appearances and he was also a poet of longing, a longing usually provoked by an absence. Holden is pining for his dead brother. And the Glass family — Franny and Zooey and the others — live in the shadow of their brother Seymour, who killed himself. It makes a kind of sense that my interest in Doris went from passing to intense because of a scene in which she herself was not present. One day in 1972, Salinger dashed into Bloomingdale's to stock up on smoked salmon before driving back up to his rural New Hampshire home. He was in the presence of his girlfriend at the time, who wondered why he didn't go upstairs to say hello to his sister.

"A little bit of my relatives goes a long way" was all he said to her.

When I first read this I thought it was disingenuous. Joyce Maynard, who describes the scene in her memoir, was nineteen at the time, and Salinger was fifty-three. That seems reason enough for not wanting to introduce her to his sister, at least not in the middle of work. But the very fact that Doris was upstairs as he dashed in and out seems poignant. In the Glass family stories, the mother is portrayed as hungry for her son's correspondence and news. She is portrayed as insatiable for this, in fact, and for this reason her son Zooey is in a constant state of mortified retreat. This theme plays itself out in many of Salinger's stories, the reticent brother and son who doesn't keep in touch.

The memories called up by Kenny Karlstein's accent took me to a place I knew from J.D. Salinger's stories and informed me about Doris Salinger's real life, which comes full circle to intersect with my own life. For all of my childhood, well into my twenties, I spent Christmas at a party given by family friends, who were Jewish, as I was, along with most of the guests. It was a big party and my attention was mostly on the kids my age, but

I recall that whenever we arrived a bunch of older people — we thought of them as the dumplings — were already ensconced in the living room watching the proceedings.

In some ways growing up is an act of understanding the lives of such people long ago, which has helped in the writing of a biography of someone of my parents' generation. Among the dumplings was a woman named Fritzi, the aunt of Don Meyers, who hosted the party with his wife, Helen. They were both psychoanalysts and colleagues of my father at the Columbia Psychoanalytic Institute. Don had been orphaned, more or less, as a young boy, and his aunt Fritzi had seen him through boarding school and college.

"My aunt Fritzi was my mother's younger sister," Don explained. "My mother was a paranoid schizophrenic, and when I was two she was hospitalized. The family had hidden from my father that she had been treated at Hillside. Very beautiful, very talented, she sang, played the piano, had a debut at one of the halls connected to Carnegie, and then she got married and withdrew from that. So Fritzi, who was childless, and married to a husband who had been very wealthy, but lost all their money during the Depression, as my mother's family also did — Fritzi went into business, and she was a very successful businesswoman.

"When I came in from boarding school I would stay with her. She had connections all over the city. She was the strong one. If anyone needed anything they went to Fritzi."

When Don was doing his psychiatric residency in New York, she would take him out to dinner with her peers, other strong, successful women, often buyers. One of these was Doris Salinger. I asked about Doris.

"She was a good-looking woman, a businesswoman. Very outgoing. She and my aunt were very fond of each other."

This was in 1951, just after Doris had gone through her second divorce. That was the year that her brother invited her on a road trip to go house shopping in New England, a trip that resulted in his buying a house on a rural New Hampshire road that would be his home for nearly sixty years, until his death in 2010.

"Did she talk about her brother?" I asked.

Apparently, she did.

"She said it was very strange that he didn't communicate," Don said. "She used to complain that he was completely isolated. She was quite the opposite. I think she used to talk to me about him because she knew I was a psychiatrist. I had already read *Catcher in the Rye*. I think I read it before I met her. She really wanted to share this with me. She was troubled by it. She was very puzzled, as though she was wondering what went wrong."

I found this both sad and exhilarating. Sad because of Doris's longing for her brother. Exhilarating to contemplate these strong, resilient women, bonded together, going to dinners and shows, independent, and reflected hereafter in the work of her brother, whose love seemed to manifest itself only in the close attention he paid to the physical world in which she lived and moved.

28

Joyce Maynard

S ALINGER'S SEDUCTION of Joyce Maynard was done by letter. She wrote an essay that appeared on the front page of the *New York Times,* accompanied by a photograph of herself as a freshman at Yale. Amid the sacks of mail that arrived in response, one letter stood out. It was from Salinger.

In her book *At Home in the World* she writes that for twenty-five years she had felt too enthralled by Salinger, in love with him in a way, even after their breakup, to write about him. She also anticipated a backlash against her for betraying his privacy. But what motivated her to write her book, in the end, was that her own daughter was coming to the age she had been when she started her affair with Salinger as a freshman in college. She was going to do for her daughter what no one, including her mother, had done for her.

Maynard is one of those writers whose talent is imbued with a blind spot that both negates the talent and may, in some way, be its source — she can describe her own actions but cannot see herself.

Her nine-month affair with Salinger took place when she was nineteen and he was fifty-three. He was no longer referring to young women as "little girls" as he did in various letters in his youth, where he alludes to how he often proposes to "little girls" and they often say yes. (The beats of the line echo, slightly, that lovely opening of "Slight Rebellion off Madison": "While riding in Fifth Avenue buses, girls who knew Holden often thought they saw him walking past Saks' or Altman's or Lord & Taylor's, but it was usually somebody else.")

Maynard writes in the present tense, and through the large swaths of the book where she relates events that happen to her, there is a two-dimensional quality to her writing; it is a bit breathless and flat. But the book's strength is the long, vivid, and complex passages treating her parents and her relationship with them. These parental passages are portraits of denial — her mother's denial in particular, as it relates to her father's shortcomings, problems, and illnesses, of which alcoholism is the most prominent. A perverse irony about that book is that all the attention it got was because of what she had to say about J.D. Salinger, but its greatest value was probably in an anatomy of one mother's relationship to her daughter, and the failings of that mother. Probably the single biggest crime Maynard's mother commits is when she reads Maynard's diary; she finds an entry in which her twelve-year-old daughter complains about her father, laments her father. When Maynard next picked up the diary she found not just evidence that it had been read, but a note, a kind of annotation or letter in which the intruder directly addresses her. The message, stated clearly, is that Maynard is wrong about her father, because she is emphasizing the tiny percentage of her father's character that is negative, and not taking into account all the good things about him. Maynard's mother is censoring her daughter for the crime of criticizing her father. "Suck it up" is the message. I am reminded of that shocking bit of advice Takoohi Saroyan gives her three-year-old son, William, when she drops him off at the orphanage — it's not enough to separate from him like this, to leave him alone, but her parting words, "don't cry," are not soothing but admonishing. If this is the greatest single sin committed by Joyce Maynard's mother, it is connected to the second-greatest sin, which is having done nothing to intervene when a fifty-three-year-old world-famous author seduced her nineteen-year-old daughter by letter, causing her to drop out of school and out of life altogether to live with him in his mountain retreat. What makes this so powerful is that Maynard does not overstate the case; she barely has to make it.

Her father was an English professor at the University of New Hampshire and a frustrated artist. Her mother was a frustrated professor — quite sympathetic in many ways, thwarted by the horrible social conventions of postwar America, almost a poster girl for the cultural claustrophobia against which Salinger was writing — who achieved a great deal in the debased but at least remunerative world of writing for women's magazines. The dynamic of her parents' hesitancy to intervene clearly had something to do with their own ambivalent relationship to the subject of fame and artistic accomplishment.

What she doesn't examine in her book is the degree to which her parents might have been afraid of her. Afraid of her drive, her willpower, her savvy. She had already eclipsed them utterly in the professional world at the ripe age of eighteen, when she appeared on the cover of the *New York Times Magazine,* cute, fresh-faced, and like Esmé, she realized later, wearing a man's watch on her thin wrist. Not just a cover model, she was author and subject — her essay, "An 18-Year-Old Looks Back on Life," was about her generation: the Now Generation, as it would come to be called.

Maynard doesn't fully plumb her own complicity in her parents' hesitancy to intervene on her behalf. When it comes it feels too late — Salinger, having gone along with her desire to have a baby, tells her he feels otherwise when they are on vacation in Florida. There is a confrontation on the beach. She flies back alone and returns to the empty house in New Hampshire to get her stuff. Her mother drives up to help gather her daughter and her daughter's things; she dresses up for the occasion, wearing fancy high boots. Maynard describes watching her trip through the deep snow in her outfit to get to the front door. For me this was an exceedingly strange image. It wasn't clear if her mother was, on some unconscious level, jazzed at the prospect of contact, however indirect, with the great man, with whom she had socialized a bit by then, but whom she was about to say goodbye to forever, even if he wasn't actually there to say goodbye to. Or maybe she was privately elated at the breakup. Maybe she had been longing for it, and had chastised herself for the whole nine-month duration of the affair for not rushing in to prevent a fateful kiss. So she had dressed up in celebration of the fact that now at last she was able to extricate her daughter from the unpleasantness with a fifty-three-year-old literary legend with strange eating habits. The reader's imagination — moral, impressionistic, literary — is provoked to all these thoughts by Maynard's description of her mother making her way through the snow.

Maynard's book cover is a photo of her as a young, blooming girl, barely a teenager, slender, flat-chested, seated on a chair, her mother behind her, voluptuous, overripe, something avid in the set of her mouth projecting intelligence and ambition, though whether for herself or the young girl is ambiguous. Stanley Kubrick, casting his Lolita, would have paused over this pair to consider them. Salinger's gift to her — in a very, very roundabout way — was to provide a kind of lure for readers who, intrigued by what they might learn about him, learn instead that Maynard can really write, at least about other people.

When Salinger moved to Cornish he spent his first year or so in a happy state of sociability with the local teenagers. He became one of their gang. When *Time*'s reporters descended on Cornish, they canvassed the town thoroughly but were met with reticence for the most part. According to Hamilton, Mel Elfin of *Newsweek* had come through town promising to quote everyone off the record and had instead used names. The result was that Salinger had switched his grocery and his hardware store, cut off communication with some people or just made the exchanges as clipped as possible.

Still, a number of young women spoke to *Time,* and they all shared a feeling of trepidation on the part of their parents regarding Salinger. Except the anxiety wasn't about his taking advantage of them; it was about his using them in his writing. Whether this fear was merely a cover for the sexual fear, or whether the idea of being "used" in someone's literary efforts somehow echoed or mirrored being used and taken advantage of in the sexual sense, I'm not sure. Maybe both.

29

1945: The End of the War

S ALINGER CHECKED himself into a hospital in Nuremberg in July 1945, increasingly disoriented and depressed. "He ached from head to foot, all zones of pain seemingly interdependent. He was rather like a Christmas tree whose lights, wired in series, must all go out if even one bulb is defective" ("For Esmé").

Kenneth Slawenski, author of *J.D. Salinger: A Life,* describes his ordeals thus:

> On April 22, after a surprisingly difficult fight for the town of Rothenberg, the path of Salinger's division brought it into a triangular region approximately 20 miles on each side, situated between the Bavarian cities of Augsburg, Landsberg, and Dachau. This territory held a series of 123 internment camps that together formed the Dachau concentration camp system, places whose stench, according to eyewitnesses, could be smelled 10 miles away.

> In the next days, between April 23 and April 28, the unit would be stationed in five different towns that housed a subcamp of Dachau.

> On April 28, after traveling through Augsburg, Salinger was likely stationed at Bobingen, the site of both divisional and regimental headquarters, just 12 and 9 miles north of the infamous camps at Landsberg and Kaufering IV.

On April 30, the day Hitler killed himself in Berlin, the 12th Regiment crossed the Amper River at Wildenroth, midway between Landsberg and the main death camp at Dachau. This route brought Salinger's division through the area of Haunstetten, the site of one of the largest subcamps in all of Germany and the location of a huge Messerschmitt factory worked by slave labor.

Slawenski notes that the daily regimental reports were written in a mode of understatement so extreme that "it was as though their authors were in a state of shock."

The personal diary of a member of the 552nd Field Artillery Battalion, which was connected with the Twelfth Infantry Regiment at the time, manages only slightly more detail:

> When the gates swung open we got our first look at the prisoners. Many of them were Jews. They were wearing black and white striped prison suits and round caps. A few had shredded blanket rags draped over their shoulders . . .
> The prisoners struggled to their feet after the gates were opened. They shuffled weakly out of the compound. They were like skeletons — all skin and bones.[1]

Salinger never tried to evoke any of this. As with much of his war experience, and in solidarity with many other soldiers and concentration camp prisoners, he felt that what he had seen was never to be spoken of again. But as a counterintelligence officer he was the first person to walk into a just-liberated concentration camp.

"You never get the smell of burning flesh out of your nose entirely, no matter how long you live," he remarked to his daughter.

---

1 Diary of Sergeant Ichiro Imamura, April 29, 1945, cited in Slawenski, originally quoted in Pierre Moulin, *Dachau, Holocaust, and US Samurais: Nisei Soldiers First in Dachau?* (Bloomington, IN: AuthorHouse, 2007), p. 125.

As one can see in Salinger's war story "A Boy in France," and as we know from the vast literature of soldiers in the field, the horror of war was commingled with all sorts of artifacts, physical and emotional, sent from home. In the case of Salinger, he received woolen socks knitted by his mother every week. "Saved my life," he told his daughter. Nearly forty-five thousand troops were taken off the front line that winter due to trench foot.

Salinger's war included colorful interludes — he was part of the liberation of Paris on August 25, among the first American troops to enter the city. He wrote to Whit Burnett describing the scene, which included Parisians rushing up to soldiers with glasses of Armagnac. He met Hemingway in Paris and they discussed Salinger's "The Last Day of the Last Furlough," which Hemingway had asked to see. A curious thing to imagine, Hemingway reading over that description of the mother watching her son in his bedroom, having brought him milk and cake, "Loving, watching." And yet Hemingway and Salinger would each write about the overwhelmed emotional state of soldiers who had seen the horrors of war and were now trying to reconcile them with the landscape of home, which had become strange in light of what they now knew.

After Paris came two successive battles that are legendary for their brutality and loss of life: the Battle of Hürtgen Forest, followed by the Battle of the Bulge, during which, Margaret writes in her memoir, *Dream Catcher,*

Salinger's friends and family feared him dead or captured. December 26 brought a call to Mrs. Salinger[2] with the news that "Sa-

---

2 One of the peculiarities of *Dream Catcher* is the way Salinger lapses into the mode of a dispassionate biographer, as she does here. I find this evocation compelling — the anxiety followed by the relief at the call — but at the same time I am filled with questions and wonder why Margaret does not address them, first and foremost among them being: What about Solomon? Was he there

linger is all right." New Year's Day, 1945, was Staff Sergeant Salinger's twenty-sixth birthday. Of this day and the following three months, the division commander writes:

On those days, melting snow revealed the bodies of both German and American soldiers upon the ground where they had been frozen into weird shapes after they had fallen in the winter battles. Hundreds of dead cattle littered the fields and destroyed vehicles lined the roads along with the carcasses of the horses that had been used to pull enemy supply vehicles. Most of the small towns had been either partially or completely destroyed and the wreckage lay untouched where it fell. Human excreta was deposited in the corners of rooms where the fighting had been at such close quarters that even leaving the building was an invitation to death. This part of Germany, just north of the point where the borders of Germany, France, and Belgium meet, was the filthiest area the 12th had ever fought through.

He ended the war near Nuremberg. On May 5, having concluded just days before what was to be its last battle, "the Twelfth Infantry Regiment opened its command post in Hermann Göring's castle at Neuhaus." The area was in chaos: Liberated displaced persons numbered in the thousands, and counterintelligence staff members, such as J.D. Salinger, were "kept extremely busy."

Just like Sergeant X in "For Esmé," who tries to write a letter home as a way of orienting himself and is horrified to see that he can't read his own handwriting, Salinger's handwriting underwent a massive change, according to his daughter, who wrote of the experience of reading the letters from this time. "The change

fretting? Did he get on the phone? Was he there as well? Solomon is the invisible man.

in my father's handwriting in the letters (which I read in the Library of Congress collection) he wrote to friends and family stateside after his release from the hospital at Nürnberg is truly spooky. His handwriting, almost as distinctive and familiar to me as his face, becomes something *totally* unrecognizable."[3]

Then there is Margaret Salinger sitting in the library researching her father, a variation on the idea of the dead or absent father. He stopped talking to her when he learned of her plans to publish a memoir; and she was clearly writing a book that she felt was about her and that she had every right to tell. (A curious twist of fate was that her memoir and Joyce Maynard's memoir were published nearly back to back, in 2000 and 1998, respectively; at times, her book is in dialogue with Maynard's, which feels awkward, but then everything about Margaret Salinger feels awkward.) Her thinking about her father as though he were dead when he is alive echoes his own treatment of his father. When Jerry Salinger married Claire Douglas in Cornish, in 1955, Jerry's mother, Miriam, and sister, Doris, were present. But not Solomon. The father who was not there.

Going all the way back to the interview with Valley Forge in 1934, when Doris and Miriam accompanied him, Slawenski speculates that Sol might have, at the time, withheld his presence because he would have been identifiable as a Jew, and so his absence was a gesture of love for his son. Coupled with the news that he was not at the wedding in Cornish, this argument becomes a bit more shaky.

---

3 This is one of the many instances in her memoir where Margaret Salinger makes use of her father's famous italics, and like almost every other instance it sounds, to me, off. She just doesn't have that particular swing.

30

1945: The Nazi Bride

O N DECEMBER 30, 1945, Salinger wrote to Elizabeth Murray from Gunzenhausen, Germany, thanking her for her kind words and best wishes. He had sent her a letter announcing his marriage to a woman named Sylvia, whom no one from his life in America had ever met or, prior to the news, even heard about. Now, from his response to Murray's enthusiastic reply, one gets the sense that hers was one of the few so openhearted. One can only imagine the response of his mother to the news that he was marrying someone she had never met and, even more saliently, not returning to New York for what must have been a long-hoped-for reunion.

His relief in writing to Murray is palpable. She is someone who functions both as a friend and coconspirator and also as a good, or at least neutral, parental figure. He lavishes praise on Sylvia's "intelligence, beauty, and style."

He reaches for his deadpan absurdist humor and achieves it, somewhat creakily, saying that he and Sylvia have their necessary supply of coal and canned peanuts. (Salinger had been discharged from the army a month earlier and signed a six-month contract with the War Department.) That they had a Christmas tree and a big turkey provided by the army. (I believe that, too, because Salinger is writing on New Year's Eve, which is also the day before his birthday. I am always rooting for Salinger to have a party even as I can picture him most vividly not in its midst.) Then he explains that the local custom is to celebrate Christmas by pelting one another with rotten eggs.

He mentions that they have bought a car, a fast, sporty Škoda, and a dog named Benny, big and black, who sits on the car's running board, pointing out Nazis for him to arrest. This last bit was clearly an attempt to defuse some anxiety within himself about Sylvia's nationality and what she had been up to during the war.

Sylvia was Salinger's equal in age — she was born on April 19, 1919, in Frankfurt am Main — and she greatly eclipsed him in education. She was fluent in German, English, French, and Italian. She was an ophthalmologist who had written a dissertation titled *Unmittelbare Kreislaufwirkungen des Apomorphins,* "Immediate Circulatory Effects of Apomorphine" — a substance created by mixing hydrochloric acid and morphine. Its purpose is to induce vomiting or help kick a heroin habit. If that is not enough to make one stare into space for a moment to ponder the possibilities, there is the strange joke in one of Salinger's letters to Murray nearly five years prior about how she and her mother have to stop dealing heroin to schoolchildren.

A friend of Salinger's from the late 1940s, Leila Hadley, said that he had talked about the "odd bond" he had with Sylvia. He reported that "they were each capable of going into trances and meeting each other, holding conversations, being together in a trance, when they were physically apart. When they compared notes afterwards, they were in perfect accord, which was both thrilling and uncanny."

Several previous biographies identify her as French. The reason may have been the fake French passport Sylvia had when they traveled to New York — necessary because German nationals were not allowed to travel. The fake passport was given to her by her husband, the former counterintelligence man.

According to Doris Salinger, who among other traits (height, formidability, handsomeness) shared her brother's flair for describing style, Sylvia was "a tall, thin woman with dark hair, pale skin, and blood-red lips and nails."

"She was *very* German," Doris added, giving her niece, Margaret, "a dark look, chin tucked in, eyebrows raised as if she were peering over the top of bifocals and directly into my eyes for emphasis."

How German was she? Sylvia was a low-level Nazi. Salinger had met her as part of his duties in counterintelligence. If that isn't strange enough, during Salinger's six-month contract working with the occupying forces after the war, one of the letters he sent back home was mailed from Nuremberg, which suggests the strong possibility that he had something to do with the Nuremberg trials. So Salinger the Bar Mitzvah boy by day worked on the Nuremberg trials and by night engaged in hot sex with a beautiful ex-Nazi with a passing interest in morphine. Which is one way for a half-Jewish American soldier to recover from a nervous breakdown. Am I sensationalizing?

The next level of surrealism is that he took her home to 1133 Park Avenue. Not just to meet his parents, but to live with them.

The image of Salinger, a veteran of war, a man married to someone he had met while interrogating her, coming through the door of his childhood home with his wife to embrace his mother, and then introducing his wife, is something out of a play. It wasn't so uncommon for newly married couples to live with their parents in those days, and from his parents' perspective, having their son and his wife living with them may have evoked memories of their own similar circumstances, when Sol and Miriam had lived with his parents. Sol's parents were fiercely disapproving of Miriam — Marjorie at the time — mostly on the grounds that she wasn't Jewish. For all his antipathy to

Sol, one has to acknowledge that there is an echo of the father's matrimonial circumstances in the son's, except that Salinger, perhaps out of some unconscious competitiveness, had vastly outdone his father, who merely brought home a redheaded Scotch-German bride to meet his father. Salinger had brought home a Nazi![1]

One has to pause over the source of this shocking information, his daughter Margaret's memoir.

At the very least, Salinger had certainly found a woman who was not Jewish.

In the immediate aftermath of World War II, J.D. Salinger was becoming the successful, sought-after writer he had always wanted to be, and yet he had somehow lost his subject. Whit Burnett had persuaded him to bring out a collection of his stories, but when Burnett's backers at Lippincott shot down the deal, it left Salinger not only embittered toward Burnett but with second thoughts about the collection itself. Don Congdon at Simon and Schuster was pursuing him to bring out a book. And yet Salinger's predicament was that all of his narrative and psychic energy was focused on the very subject that he did not want to write about. The war and its wounds would be honored with silence. He had to live with the bitter irony that it is only when he finally comes home that he can fully confront the extent to which the landscape of home is shut off to him, though surely this was part of his motivation in lingering in Europe as long as he did. It was surely part of his bond with Sylvia — they had both been through something unfathomable to the people who had remained stateside. His sensitivities to the landscape of New York, whose topography had nourished his fiction, made

---

1 Then again Sol was obviously going to be more receptive to his son's non-Jewish wife than his own father had been to Miriam.

home too much to bear precisely because it would seem too strange after what he had experienced. It was out of the question that he could take his perceiving apparatus back home and live among the civilians.

It was almost a kind of double exile: first two years abroad as a witness to war. And then the self-imposed exile of consciousness, not being able to face the civilians or see, with any honesty or clarity or pleasure, the landscape of his youth. Surely this must have added to his erotic relationship with Sylvia. They were both, in some way, refugees. In several biographies the marriage broke up because of Sylvia's displeasure with her new country and her difficulty in adjusting to America. This seems like a very strange conclusion to draw; she wasn't adjusting to America, or even New York. She was adjusting to living with Miriam Salinger, who had been wishing for her son's return home for two years and was now coping with an interloper.

As usual, there's not a word said about Sol concerning this period of the two couples cohabitating. One can speculate that this is because Sol said not a word, or because nobody liked what Sol had to say.

Sylvia lasted less than a month. One morning at breakfast she found a plane ticket on her plate. Salinger decamped for Daytona Beach, Florida. On Sheraton Plaza Hotel stationery ("formerly The Clarendon") and "directly on the ocean," he writes to Elizabeth Murray, in longhand, that the marriage was a failure — he blames the participants, and says they brought each other nothing but unhappiness. I don't believe a word of it. But he often used Murray as a way to reflect his best self. At the time he must have felt it imperative to destroy any sense of romance and, hopefully, the grief that went with it.

Salinger completed two brilliant and significant stories in 1947, the year following the end of his marriage: "A Young Girl in

1941 with No Waist at All" and "A Girl I Knew." Both stories reach back to a time before the war. Both work with autobiographical experiences from a perspective the author could not have imagined when he lived them. But while "A Young Girl in 1941 with No Waist at All" is set entirely in the prelapsarian world before he saw bloody combat and the war's other horrors, "A Girl I Knew" is an attempt to bracket the trauma of the intervening years. At the end of the story John wanders through the now abandoned and desecrated home of his former, Jewish, love. "I walked to the window, opened it, and looked down for a moment at the balcony where Leah had once stood."

This is as close as Salinger, who always had a knack for omission and implication, comes to directly addressing the Holocaust in his fiction. The homeopathic strategy of using the tiniest trace of a substance to achieve maximum effect is more fully developed in the work of the second panel of the triptych, most notably in "Esmé," the story "A Girl I Knew" most directly anticipates.

But there are many kinds of battle, many arenas of innocence. It is significant that these two stories come on the heels of the end of his marriage to Sylvia, during which he hardly wrote at all. The sense I have of that marriage: tumultuous, ecstatic, sexual, and paranoid in the way that love can feel like a conspiracy of two. They have secrets they can only share with each other. One possible element of their shared secret is suggested toward the end of "A Girl I Knew." John is returning to Vienna on official business and trying to find out what happened to Leah. "Another Wiener, an unteroffizier, standing at strict attention, told me what terrible things had been done to the Jews in Vienna. As I had rarely, if ever, seen a man with a face quite so noble and full of vicarious suffering as this unteroffizier's was, just for the devil of it I had him roll up his left sleeve. Close to his armpit he had the tattooed blood-type marks of an old SS man."

The words "I had him" seem innocuous compared to the ones that immediately follow, "the blood-type marks of an old SS man." But I find them significant. Salinger's heroes, most notably Holden, are usually powerless, without authority. They are children, in some way, even as adults. But Staff Sergeant Salinger of the Counter Intelligence Corps had considerable authority. He interrogated Germans, looking for Nazi officers posing as civilians.

Previous biographies have implied that one of these impostures was Sylvia herself. Some have gone so far as to speculate that she was a member of the Gestapo, and that Salinger discovered this only after they were married and living with his parents. But there is no concrete evidence of this, only that it was Salinger who sued for the divorce, claiming to have been deceived. "False representations" were the words his lawyer—his father's lawyer—used. But this seems like an unnecessary extrapolation. It is enough to note that an American sergeant in charge of interrogating Germans, and with the authority to "have" them do as he wished, married a German woman, and took her back home to New York.

It was a shock to discover in Margaret Salinger's memoir that Sylvia wrote to Salinger many years later. Even more shocking is Margaret's report of her father getting into the car in front of the post office in Windsor, New Hampshire, with the letter in his hand, looking at it, and then tearing it up without opening it. Early in his life, way back in 1941, Salinger had written to Murray excitedly that he was wrapping up a new short story, but was having difficulty with the ending. He remarked that endings are hard; there really are no endings. As a form of literary foreshadowing, knowing the turn his work would take as it tunneled into the privacy of his bunker, literally and figuratively, this is poignant. But when it came to his relationships with other people, he was capable of endings, and they were decisive and final. This would come to include the one he had with his daughter. When Margaret was asked on a talk show if she could describe her current relationship with her father, she said it was easy. "There is none."

31

1961: The Year of the Woodchuck

I N T H E F A L L O F 1 9 6 1 *Time* put J.D. Salinger on its cover
to coincide with the publication of *Franny and Zooey*. The
article's first paragraph contained five sentences, the last of
which read: "Not long ago, when he and his family were away, a
couple of neighbors could stand it no longer, put on dungarees
and climbed over the 6½-ft. fence to take a look around."

The media's neurotic relationship to J.D. Salinger reaches
its zenith in this line. You have to focus on the "it." The man's
neighbors were being afflicted by something that they could not
tolerate any longer. Neighbors get on each other's nerves for all
kinds of reasons. For example:

- They play loud music.
- They have dogs that bark incessantly.
- They yell and scream and make noise.
- They walk around naked and make you see things you
  would rather not.
- They are weirdly rude to you when you see them.
- They act like you are a criminal or a freak for no good rea-
  son.
- They shoot guns.
- They have political beliefs that you find repulsive.
- They trespass on your property, or spy on you, or invade
  your personal space in some way.

Maybe, *maybe* you could put on this list: They keep to themselves. And if it qualifies it is at the very bottom of the list. Keeping to himself is the "it" that had become unbearable to the point where his neighbors had to scale a fence and trespass on his property while he was away. Salinger hadn't invited them into his home and his life, so they were forced to break in.

The lead paragraph's first four lines, about how he was outgoing when he arrived and now he is not, would be hilarious in their dishonest scandal mongering if it weren't for the fact that the taint of McCarthyism was still in the air, for which *Time* has to take some responsibility; the insinuating-guilt-by-implication mode in which any weirdness is a possible clue that leads to . . . I don't know, to what? Treachery, treason, communism, veganism, deviant sexual behavior.

Forward ran the innuendos in that particular *Time* magazine style. Mr. and Mrs. Walter Jenks, the fence-jumping neighbors, were real people, but their actions personify *Time*'s approach to Salinger — the man had something to hide. It would be a template for years to come. The subtext of *Time*'s approach is summed up in one of the dispatches sent in by the team of reporters working on the case: "We have found a lead that may have finally opened up Mr. Salinger's closet of little girls."

Salinger's face is featured on the cover as an illustration — a somewhat handsome if dour, possibly troubled-looking Salinger in middle age set against a field of rye. The artist has imbued him with the pastiness of a sexual deviant.[1]

---

1 A complicating twist to *Time*'s treatment of Salinger was that it was overseen by Henry Grunwald, who would later go on to be managing editor of *Time* and then editor in chief of Time Inc., but in 1961 he was in charge of the magazine's book coverage. He would assemble a book of critical essays about Salinger that came out in 1962, and seemed to be engaged and, in a word, a fan. But somehow he felt he had to approach Salinger not as an author with a unique and

Cornish, New Hampshire, was overrun by journalists and woodchucks in 1961. The first of the journalists arrived in 1960, when *Newsweek* sent a team in to report a feature. The occasion wasn't the appearance of a Salinger book but the opposite — it had been seven years since *Nine Stories*. The work Salinger had published in *The New Yorker* was widely discussed but hardly available; the issue with "Franny" had been sold out for years. The aura of samizdat Salinger had already emerged, but it was focused on the scarcity of the work. It had not yet pivoted to the scarcity of the author.[2]

In terms of the books, we are only halfway through the second panel of the triptych, but chronologically it is the home stretch. "A Perfect Day for Bananafish" had come out in 1948. There are only three years left before all the work was published in book form and the third panel begins.

The locals were comparatively relaxed about talking to the first reporter who showed up in town, *Newsweek*'s Mel Elfin. One quote stands out, by Salinger's soon-to-be-former friend Bertram Yeaton, who described Salinger's workday: "He woke

---

puzzling gift, but as a scandal in the making. Which in itself may speak to the force of the undertow of the celebrity-industrial complex, and Salinger's prescience in wanting to avoid it at all costs. Which then leads to the question: If you want to avoid it at all costs, is the best way to go about this to avoid it at all costs?

2 Something about Salinger's recusal seems to immobilize the intelligence of even a highly literate, close reader such as Ian Hamilton, never mind the rest of the media and the Biography Corps, who speculate on why Salinger was up in the woods with all the nuance and insight of a two-year-old having a temper tantrum. It has been suggested that this was some of kind of intentional strategy for increasing interest in his work. The idea that he both wanted to have his work widely read and also to be left alone is unimaginable. The whole "what is he doing up there?" mystery has been a distraction from the much more interesting mysteries surrounding Salinger and his work: What does his writing provoke in us? How does it achieve this effect, and why?

between 5:00 and 6:00 a.m. and walked down the hill to his studio, a tiny concrete shelter with a translucent plastic roof. He would put in up to 16 hours a day.

"Jerry works like a dog," Yeaton said. "He's a meticulous craftsman who constantly revises, polishes and rewrites. On the wall of his studio, Jerry has a series of cup hooks to which he clips sheaves of notes. They must deal with various characters and situations, because when an idea occurs to him, he takes down the clip, makes the appropriate notation and places it back on the proper hook. He also has a ledger in which he has pasted sheets of typewritten manuscript on one page and on the others he has arrows, memos, other notes for revisions."

This passage brought me up short and took me straight to Salinger's story "The Varioni Brothers," published in the *Saturday Evening Post* in 1943, about two brothers who are wildly successful songwriters until one of them is shot by a mobster, who had intended to kill the other one. It's an interesting story without being a great story, but the thematic seams that would later be sewn into the work much more expertly are broadly visible here. It also seemed to say something about the way Salinger's mind operated as he composed his stories. I had been so intrigued by the fastidious neatness of his typescripts — the stories themselves, and the letters, too — because their professionalism seemed to camouflage their process almost as much as word processing software does to composition today (almost — the typewriter is still pretty expressive; not all periods get punched with the same force).

The story's plot is complicated by the fact that the brother who writes the music enjoys the trappings of success, while the one who writes the lyrics doesn't. He wants to be working on his novel. At first this seems like an allegory of the two sides of J.D. Salinger: the writer who wants to sell to the slicks, sell to Hollywood, be a star, and the serious writer who is devoted to his craft. One of the brothers — the one who writes the music and likes the high life — is called Sonny. He's the one the mobster had intended to shoot, and in his grief and guilt he drops everything and devotes his whole life to "typing up the manuscript of a lovely, wild and possibly great novel. It was written and thrown into a trunk by Joe Varioni. It was written longhand on yellow paper, on lined paper, on crumpled paper, on torn paper. The sheets were not numbered. Whole sentences and even paragraphs were marked out and rewritten on the backs of envelopes, on the unused sides of college exams, in the margins of railroad timetables."

After *Newsweek* came Ed Kosner and the *New York Post,* and then Ernest Havemann writing for *Life.* Then came *Time's* juggernaut. Reporters and stringers filed dispatches from New York, Washington, D.C., Florida, London, Jamaica, and Los Angeles. Several were dispatched to Cornish itself.

In another narrative of success — Elvis, the Beatles — the drumbeat of dispatches would be exciting to witness, fame would beget fame, the record shoots to the top of the charts. But in the context of Salinger it was like an assault. Even the landscape's imagery was suggestive of battle — Salinger ensconced in his fort at the top of the hill while interlopers came scurrying up the mountain in the hopes of breaching his defenses.

The tone and style of these dispatches range from the staccato rhythms of a dictated telegram to leisurely literary excursions typed out on onionskin paper that practically qualify as literary essays in their own right. Much of the material is fascinating as an example of how *Time* practiced journalism in 1961. From Jamaica, where socialite Leila Hadley had been interviewed, we have the following:

HE WROTE ON AN ARTISTS DRAWING BOARD BUT I AM
NOT CERTAIN IF HE SPURNED TYPEWRITERS ENTIRELY
AND WROTE BY HAND STOP WE DISCUSSED TRAVEL AS

I GOING ON WORLD TRIP HE THOUGHT WHOLE THING
POINTLESS THAT TRAVEL ITSELF OFFERED ABSOLUTELY
NOTHING STOP.

Benny, who rode along with Sylvia and Jerry in Germany after their marriage pointing at Nazis to arrest, made the trip back
to New York. According to testimony from his publisher in
London, in 1954, "He was living with a huge black shaggy dog
nearly as big as himself. When he wasn't writing he was franti-
cally exercising [the] dog around streets."

One soldier who had worked with him in counterintelligence reports that they were colleagues but not friends and then
adds, provocatively,

EYE WAS FROM POOR PEOPLE AND HE WAS FROM RICH
PEOPLE. WE GENERALLY GOT ALONG ON AYE LIVE AND
LET LIVE BASIS. IN MY OPINION HE WOULD LOOK DOWN
ON ME AND I SOMETIMES THOUGHT HE WAS A LITTLE
BELIGERANT.

But then another soldier, Jack Alturas, had a different take
and seemed to have gone through much of the war with Salinger, having "made the D-Landing on June 6th together; they
were among the first to enter Paris on Aug 25th served together
through Belgium, Luxemburg, and Germany. He was from Park
Avenue, but there wasn't anything park avenue about him that
suggested park avenue. He was just a nice guy."

Don Congdon had been a friend of Salinger's and one of
his champions during the postwar years; as a fiction editor at
Collier's he had fought so hard for a Salinger story that his boss
said that if Congdon put the story on his desk one more time he
was fired. He later tried to sign up *The Catcher in the Rye* for Simon and Schuster. In the late forties Salinger would often join a
poker game at Congdon's place on Charlton Street, after which

he would head to Chumley's for a nightcap. When a *Time* editor called to ask Congdon if he would be interviewed for their article, he said no, "because Jerry cherished his privacy."

Over the next few weeks I was called twice more. The last caller sounded like a young man. He said he had a special assignment to see me about Jerry, and when I said I would not meet him, he said it would mean his job if I didn't see him; I said too bad, he would be at the unemployment office the next day. Because of so much pressure, it occurred to me that I should write Jerry a note and advise him that I had refused to talk to *Time*. He wrote back, expressing his thanks, which was the last communication between us.

While *Time* sent its agents into the field, Salinger was working the phones and shoring up defenses. It's almost like a thriller until I consider what it might feel like to think that nearly everyone you had ever met was going to be contacted by people who did not have your interests in mind. The whole thing seems like something from *Dragnet* — diligent, raincoat-clad police detectives tracking down the criminal.

Here the specter of Ian Hamilton rears up, unflatteringly for Hamilton, because the natural response to this overkill is to ask: For what crime?

Any levelheaded examination of *Time*'s pursuit and agenda would have to conclude that there is something imbalanced about them, but *Time* didn't become a gigantic moneymaking magazine by being demure; this was straitlaced scandal mongering. Rather than at least discussing the matter, Hamilton dons his own trench coat and goes with the flow.

I think of a small note written on a single fluttering index card that I came across in Ian Hamilton's papers at Princeton. Addressed to his editor, Jason Epstein, it read:

One person has talked but in conditions of high secrecy. I will give you the name when I see you, and give you the circumstances . . . I now know for certain that Salinger has been writing all these years; and I think I know, from this source, as well as one other, what is preventing him from publishing.

Conditions of high secrecy . . . This source, as well as one other . . . I now know for certain . . .
Breathless panting of someone whispering to you from an alley trying to entice you to come in.

Time's efforts unearthed two little playlets that are each in their own way dark and surreal and disturbing.

In Los Angeles, there is the spectacle of *Time* reporters finding Salinger's brother-in-law Gavin Douglas. They interviewed him twice. The first time he was "digesting a recently consumed half gallon of white wine." Their description of Gavin: "Age 30, long blond hair, mouthful of bad teeth, hypnotically steady grey blue eyes." He was incoherent, and responded to their questions with mumbling about a telegram he received from his brother-in-law that said something about his "remittance" being increased and how "he should not tell anyone anything."

Which is pretty incredible, if you want to know the truth.

The next interview a week later went better: The subject was inclined toward gratitude, because *Time's* reporters had bailed Gavin out of the drunk tank of the local jail. Therefore he was sober, though not all that lucid. He prefaced his comments with the rationalization that it was okay to talk about Salinger because "he invaded my privacy. People who know I'm related to him ask if I'm Holden Caulfield, or Seymour, or someone. Well, I'm not."

The issue of anxiety of influence takes on a whole new dimension here: Does Gavin sound like Holden because Salinger had so accurately captured the way some people — especially smart, deluded, self-destructive people — actually talk? Or was Gavin talking this way because he had read or, through contact with the author himself, otherwise imbibed the work of J.D. Salinger?

Gavin says that Salinger declared, "A writer's worst enemy is another writer."

He recounts an elaborate lie Claire told their parents after she met Salinger at a party thrown by relatives of *The New Yorker*'s Francis Steegmuller, in Manchester, Vermont, while she was attending Radcliffe. She started visiting him on weekends, reporting to her parents that he had "a big red converted barn where he kept fifteen or twenty Buddhist friends on the income from his Catcher royalties. It sounded wild and I sort of didn't believe her. Then just before she married Jerry, she told me it was all lies."

Among the tales is one that stands out for being sexy and dark: Salinger was meeting his English publishers, and played a prank on them. He met them at the Stork Club, where Claire and a friend had gone separately, "slinking in and acting like call girls. Jerry pointed them out to the publishers as examples of that kind of woman, and asked if they'd like a closer look. He asked the girls over to the table for an hour or two and they went with it, talking tough and casting sly glances at the Englishmen. I don't know if he ever told them what was really up."

It's difficult to know how to take these stories, other than as evidence of the rather brutalized childhoods that Gavin and Claire had — their parents, who came to America during the war, were obsessed with their careers as art dealers and more or less abandoned their children to a series of foster homes.

Not all of Gavin's testimony about his sister and Salinger is edged with blinking neon, though. Some is sweet. "I helped him put in a walk and some steps the first time I was there," he said of the house in Cornish. "He's very good with his hands and it interests him intensely. He's trying very hard to be self-sufficient."

The other playlet is even darker. For a fleeting moment *Time* thinks it has found the Salinger closet and its most famous little girl: the girl on whom Sybil, from "A Perfect Day for Bananafish," is modeled. Or maybe it's Esmé? She is neither, it turns out. Their lead is all wrong. But it is a thread the editors nevertheless worry. Salinger met the girl, Jean Miller, in 1950, in a Daytona, Florida, resort.³ She wasn't three, or thirteen, she was fifteen. There had been a friendship between the young girl and the older man, but had there been a romance? Her parents had intervened in Florida, but was it in time?

Time interviewed her father, "a corset-maker, soap-maker and banker of Cortland, New York." The report quotes him describing Salinger: "He was an odd fellow. He didn't mingle much with other guests. He fastened onto Jean [who was sixteen or seventeen at the time], and spent a lot of time with her. He was — well, is he Jewish? I thought that explain[ed] how he acted. Oh, I mean I thought he might have a chip on his shoulder. The fact that he didn't mingle much, I mean."

A year later, "when the family came to New York City, they invited Salinger to dinner."⁴

---

3 Salinger is not alone in finding vacation travel fertile ground for intrigue, but after immersing oneself in his life and work one becomes sensitized to the various meanings of the words "cruise" and "cruising." Also, Daytona is where he went, alone, in 1947 after his marriage with Sylvia broke up, and where he would later take Joyce Maynard twenty-five years later and break up with her.

4 A year later places this encounter in 1951, the year *The Catcher in the Rye* was published. I am reminded of the road trip Salinger took with his sister, Doris, looking for a house in the country. Doris is most vivid to us through Margaret Salinger's book, and as a firsthand witness to J.D. Salinger's youth her attitudes have special importance. Margaret frames her whole book with a long discus-

When *Time* reporters confronted the girl in 1961, she was by then a married woman: the moment for the drama of a courtroom confrontation had finally come. *Time* reporter Bill Smith's report reads:

> J. tried to be aloof ... Didn't remember where she had met Salinger or what he was like. Well, did she deny that she, as a child, had known him in Florida? She puffed on her cigarette a moment, as if debating over which plea to enter: "Yes," she said carefully, "I think I do deny it."

Meanwhile, back in Cornish, a reporter named Murphy files a lengthy and rather lapidary account of the current scene. "The easiest way to engage a Yankee in conversation is just drop the name Woodchuck," he writes. It's a major preoccupation for the whole town. Claire Douglas Salinger is duly preoccupied: "About three weeks before I got up there, she could be seen in Hanover two or three times a week, in hardware stores or just talking with people on the street getting advice on woodchucks."

There is a description of the Salinger garden with its "three or four rows of corn, some tomatoes and a root plant," sur-

---

sion of anti-Semitism and its effects on her father's worldview, all based on cross-references to Doris's stories with her own reading and research. At times I feel her reading of all this is overstated. For example, she insists that the reason Salinger so hated anything Ivy League is because the academy was filled with anti-Semites. Not untrue, exactly, but that didn't stop many Jewish intellectuals of the same generation from becoming literary critics, and sometimes academics, too, Alfred Kazin being an example of the former. Still, an anecdote like the one above lingers. Salinger made Holden Caulfield Catholic and his grandfather's funny accent — which in Salinger's life would have been a Yiddish accent — Australian. I think Margaret has a point in being incredulous about this choice and thinking it was in some ways a defensive act.

rounded by a fence three feet high composed of sticks and wire. Then the solitary declarative phrase: "Against the woodchucks."

It's unclear whether *Time*'s project was to fact-check Salinger's fiction against his life and thereby demystify him, or if it was performing the journalistic equivalent of the Starr report, in the hopes of uncovering some lewd, salacious, and possibly illegal activity that would bring the whole empire crashing down. But what empire? There were many writers more explicitly politically subversive than J.D. Salinger in the previous decades. Salinger's writing was subversive, but not for a reason that could be identified. Perhaps this is what goaded *Time* — the vexing feeling that there was something there that couldn't be explained.

The word "searching" is so commonly used in connection with J.D. Salinger that it feels like a cliché. The literal interpretation of what is being sought is J.D. Salinger himself, up on his mountain, behind his fence. But his reclusiveness, though it surely stoked curiosity, is more of a convenient metaphor than an end in itself. There is something about Salinger's writing that creates, in his readers, a sense of their being on a quest of some kind. To read him was to be in search of a hidden riddle. The riddle wasn't some coded spiritual message or obscure instruction on how to live. These were present in the surface of the writing but they were false leads. The mystery was why his prose pleased them. The quest was for the source of their pleasure. It was that alchemical mix of seduction, flattery, and the sense of mortal danger. It was both in the writing and between the lines. Writing had no business making you feel that way, was the unstated remark beneath the curiosity about Salinger.

32

1972: "Begin the Beguine"

THERE IS A haunting scene in Joyce Maynard's memoir in which she talks of dancing to "Begin the Beguine" with Salinger in his living room in Cornish, where she was now living. The moment, like the relationship, was romantic and perverse. Salinger had mentioned this tune in his Ursinus column, "Musings of a Social Soph: The Skipped Diploma," more than thirty years earlier, when it was a popular hit.

She describes the moment with such intimacy, aware that the two of them were doing something unique, which is a safe enough bet—probably not many couples, romantically involved but not having sexual intercourse (her body refused to cooperate for the act), aged fifty-three and nineteen, were dancing to "Begin the Beguine" in mountaintop living rooms in New Hampshire in 1972. What is so interesting about this moment is partly the sense of intimacy Maynard feels sharing this dance with Salinger, and also an awareness that the song and the moment have an entirely different set of associations for him than for her. This is Maynard's first time around dancing to "Begin the Beguine." But it's not Jerry Salinger's. His wish to keep dancing to an old tune raises the question: What world was he so happy to revisit when listening to it? The song made its splash when Artie Shaw recorded it in 1938. By 1940 it was a standard of big bands. Was this one of the songs Salinger listened to in Vienna with the daughter of his host family? Was it one of the two records that John and Leah play over and over in "A Girl I Knew"? Or was this one of the songs he heard and danced to in 1940, that triumphant year of his first publication in *Story,* and then his cruise ship adventure? Or perhaps it was what was playing when he danced with Oona O'Neill at the Stork Club. Or all of the above.

Maynard's book came out in 1998. Two years later Margaret Salinger published *Dream Catcher.* Her book is difficult to read at times, in part because we are witnessing the sadness, pain, and frustration about her relationship with her father in which she feels secondary to his fictional world — it's almost as though he were keeping a second family in his working hutch apart from the house, and liked them better. But this sense of exclusion has a component of resentment at being deprived not just of her father's attention but of his artistic patrimony. She doesn't have the music in her prose — the early parts of the book are strewn with quotations from Shakespeare, Shelley, Byron, as though she is calling in literary reinforcements.

When I came across the italicized *"totally"* quoted earlier, I was reminded of this. By sensitivity I do not mean emotional sensitivity but artistic sensitivity; the kind, for example, that makes a fetish out of italicizing words, or even parts of words, and somehow creates a kind of music out of it. Margaret's use of *totally,* trying to evoke her father's radically changed handwriting in the aftermath of his war trauma, feels clumsy in comparison.

Why should one be concerned about such a thing — a word that doesn't sound quite right — when a daughter is reporting so urgently on her father, his life, and her relationship with him? Because part of her frustration with him is about just this matter of elegance and lightness of touch; she knows he has style, but style is not enough. In her vexation with her father I am reminded of her father's vexation with *his* father, of the *Ursinus Weekly* column referring to Sol as "unreasonable."

Margaret is one of these wonderfully bright people who nevertheless are missing that essential gene for navigating the world, especially other people. One heartbreaking example of this was a live online chat she did on CNN in 2000, right in the midst of the flurry of attention generated by her book. Someone named Halley writes in with a question about any regrets she may have about the book. Margaret replies: "Gosh, I wish I hadn't put in everything about drinking urine, because that's all I'm reading. It speaks to my odd upbringing that I didn't find this particularly peculiar. I never expected to see that as sort of a 'shockeroo' headline."

This lack of foresight does not speak to her odd upbringing; it speaks to something in her personality that is clueless about the world and oblivious to her own motives. Salinger is presented as a parent with many flaws but he is, as usual, capable of remarkable insight. On one occasion he says she is "cursed with a readable face." A beautiful remark; its corollary being that she is cursed with an inability to read the faces of others, or to foresee that reporting on her father's strange dietary habits would be seized on and sensationalized — red meat for the woodchucks.

On another occasion, Salinger visits Margaret at boarding school, where an administrator is tormenting her, and makes some gestures to intervene at her request; they are insufficient, in her view. Then he moves on to encouraging her, over dinner, to enjoy her piece of chocolate cake. On one hand this is an evasion of his daughter's complaint, and on the other hand it is wise counsel: Enjoy your cake while it's there.

33

The Miscalculation

I T IS IMPOSSIBLE to discuss the life of J.D. Salinger without addressing his reclusiveness and its costs. When the crazies came out of the woodwork waving their copies of *The Catcher in the Rye,* they were conspicuous in part because if you assassinate an international figure, or try to, and then announce your favorite novel, it will get attention. But they were also operating in a vacuum. By exiling everyone else he left himself with the crazy people. By not talking to any journalists at all, and by making it a cause of excommunication for anyone else in his life to talk to a journalist about him, he forfeited the field to speculation. Of course it is an impossible situation — you can't dignify terrible slander by responding to it. And yet in a vacuum some rumors will simply grow unchecked.

I spoke to a woman who had known Salinger — and asked that her name not be used — who presented me with the following anecdote: One day her daughter came home from her Manhattan private school and reported that the teacher had begun a conversation about *Nine Stories* by saying, "There are two things you need to know about Salinger. He was a child molester and he was a symbolist."

I paused for a long time when I heard that. "What's a symbolist?" I finally said.

"Hell if I know," said the woman. "I mean, you know, it

means that when the guy is throwing an orange in the air in 'The Laughing Man,' it's a sign of fertility. Remember that one?" I did.

"Well," she continued, "a symbolist means the teacher says that when the guy tosses an orange up in the air it means the orange is a symbol of fertility. Or you know how when the Chief's girlfriend starts showing up to the baseball games and she insists she play, and then she hits a triple? It means she's pregnant and in her third trimester."

We spend a minute being dismissive and contemptuous of this approach. The primary objection is that it sucks all the joy out of the work. This is the ingenious and maddeningly effective technique employed by the humorless: Their interpretation always sounds plausible until you remember how essential, if unquantifiable, humor is to the equation. Humor is beyond their reach. The magnificently perceptive (and funny) critic Wilfrid Sheed wrote, " 'A Perfect Day for Bananafish,' for instance, only works because Seymour Glass is so funny; likewise, 'For Esmé with Love and Squalor' manages to steer its treacherous course between sentimentality and case history entirely by grace of the narrator's throwaway lines, and Salinger's own uproarious imitation of Esmé — which incidentally does not depend on his famous italicized dialogue, which is sometimes discussed as if it were his sole comic resource."

Having disposed of symbolism, the woman and I are left with the other accusation. There is a moment of silence.

"Why would a teacher say that?" I said. "I mean, yes, kissing a three-year-old girl's foot on the beach when her parents are not around is not a good thing. But that is fiction, for one thing. And being a serial seducer of college-age girls does start to look ugly after a while but I wouldn't call it . . ."

"I think he miscalculated," she said. "I think Jerry miscalculated in the way he played his reclusiveness out and his wonderful sense of privacy."

"What do you mean?"

"I think he understood a problem so deeply and so early—this problem of the corruption that goes with celebrity—but he miscalculated when you infuriate the press. Sure, be careful about who can talk about you. But if you tell everyone near you to shut up, who does that leave telling your story? The person who tells the story is totally on the outside." There was a pause. "That strange trinity of him and [William] Shawn and Lillian [Ross], and this strange ethic of silence that they talked themselves into. Writing is an action. There is an aggression in it."

34

Gustave Lobrano and William Shawn

FOR ALL OF my enthusiasm for the first panel of the triptych, there is no question that Salinger's work is in some fundamental way changed when it begins to appear in *The New Yorker,* starting with "A Perfect Day for Bananafish" in 1948. The stories are leaner, lighter, and pack a stronger punch. The biggest weakness of the early stories was that some of the best ones tended to drift a little bit; their endings seemed a bit loose and baggy. The endings of the *New Yorker* stories are much stronger. So are the beginnings. In short, Salinger's work is benefiting from the editing for which *The New Yorker* is famous, and infamous.

But who deserves credit for this editing?

In the literature of *The New Yorker* — that parade of memoirs and biographies written by the many contributors to the magazine — Gus Lobrano's name usually comes up in the context of the brief flurry of anxious maneuvering that took place in the aftermath of Harold Ross's unexpected death in 1951. In these accounts Lobrano is mentioned as having contended for the editorship, which went to William Shawn. Gustave Lobrano is left to an almost Rosencrantz and Guildenstern–like fate somewhere offstage — a reader is left to imagine a figure pacing his office, making harrumphing sounds of displeasure about not getting the top job.

But working on this book has revealed an entirely different

figure. Gus Lobrano and William Shawn are the two editors[1] who most directly influenced Salinger's published work.

Lobrano took over the fiction department in 1938, when Katharine White moved to Maine. Wolcott Gibbs sent him a letter to orient him to his new job: "The average contributor to this magazine is semiliterate; that is, he is ornate to no purpose, full of senseless and elegant variations, and can be relied on to use three sentences where a word would do."

Lobrano's sensibility seems to have leaned strongly toward the word that will do. His edits on "A Perfect Day for Bananafish" were extensive, with special attention to the story's opening, and it is those first paragraphs that seem like such a striking departure from what came before. When Roger Angell described the story's appearance as "like a shot," one must acknowledge the pun, but I think he meant to refer to the whole story, not just its end.

Lobrano edited Salinger up until 1956, when he died of cancer at age fifty-four. In addition to being a great editor he was known for his affable, inclusive manner with his stable of writers, who included James Thurber, S.J. Perelman, John Cheever, Irwin Shaw, and Roger Angell. He liked to pal around —"he was a very amusing, friendly man," as his daughter put it. He played tennis with some of his writers (notably Salinger and Shaw), enjoyed lunch with them, and invited them to his home. He started a neighborhood Sunday softball game in Chappaqua, and once in a while an author would take the field. Salinger became a family friend, even traveling to Boston for the wedding of Lobrano's son in 1953. He liked to bring people together. Salinger's correspondence to Lobrano is peppered with allusions

---

1 Whit Burnett could be put on this list, too, but somehow the role of discovering Salinger, even guiding him, seems different from shaping the work in the editing process, a fact that Burnett attests to when he references Salinger's highly edited first drafts.

to tennis matches they had watched together, to lunches they had shared.

Some of my information about Lobrano came from Roger Angell. But mostly he remained a mysterious figure. I was casting about for someone else with a connection to Gus Lobrano, to whom, along with his agent, Dorothy Olding, Salinger dedicated *Nine Stories.* I found a woman listed on the West Coast who seemed about the right age. I called, and found Gus Lobrano's daughter, Dorothy Lobrano Guth. It was near dinnertime on the West Coast, I was a total stranger, and she was wary, understandably. She asked me to send her a letter explaining my project, which I did.

Thus began a pursuit that lasted for the duration of my project. All her skepticism was totally reasonable — why would you tell anything to a person who called you out of the blue? — and yet there was something else. After receiving my letter she asked for an independent note from Roger Angell, a good friend of hers, which Roger graciously provided. Yet still there was a sense of avoidance and resistance.

Meanwhile, the more I researched, the more I realized that the leap in Salinger's work that occurs in 1948 is attributable to Lobrano's editing. He was the one going over the galleys with a pencil. He was the one who asked for revisions and meticulously edited the stories. He listened to Salinger's writing voice and helped shape it and put it on paper. Here was this enormously important figure who had not gotten his due!

From my current vantage point I see that it was this circumstance of Lobrano's early death that made me avid, too. I had placed Salinger on the same streets of Vienna as my father, in 1937–38. It was as though I wanted to use the occasion of my biography of Salinger — an author whose most famous metaphor was that of saving kids from falling off a cliff — to raise the dead fathers, unheralded, cut off in their prime, from their graves.

To resurrect them and hang a medal around their necks — as though that would make a difference.

I wrestled with the likelihood that Dorothy Lobrano Guth may not have wanted to talk to me in too much detail precisely because what I wanted to talk about involved the painful memory of her father's death. But the very aura of her father's death only increased that terrible feeling of people falling through time into darkness, all the ephemeral stories and experiences they carried going dark with them.

I really needed her to tell me more about her father. I wanted to tell people interested in J.D. Salinger that besides the important influence of William Shawn, "most unreasonably modest of born great artist-editors," as Salinger puts it in the dedication to *Franny and Zooey,* there was another, earlier important influence on Salinger. Many people interested in Salinger know of Shawn's importance to him. What has not been widely known is that the man who first shaped the legend was Gustave Lobrano.

Yet I knew that to betray this nearly hysterical sense of urgency to Dorothy Lobrano Guth would do nothing to reassure her of my trustworthiness. To make matters worse, she had worked at *The New Yorker* in the newsbreaks department and had edited E.B. White's letters, which is to say she had that astringent, concise sensibility to which all this emoting would be anathema.

When Gus Lobrano died of cancer in 1956, it was a surprise to everyone, including Gus Lobrano: The convention at that time was to tell the family but not the patient. "They didn't find cancer early in those days and they didn't know what to do when they did. The doctor more or less said just go home and die," said Lobrano Guth. A vague explanation was offered: Lobrano had phlebitis.

Dorothy and her family were pretending to Lobrano and to

the many well-wishers who wrote and called that all was relatively well. They concocted a story about how he would be traveling with his wife to Nassau for a recuperative vacation.

Salinger wrote to Lobrano in the hospital, not long after he
and Claire were married. The letter, dated "Sunday" [probably
1955], was a rambling prose poem that evoked Salinger's hatred
of the word "phlebitis" and offered advice as to what Lobrano
should say, or chant, at the exact moment of death for optimal
results in the afterlife. It's difficult to distinguish what part of
this is Salinger being a bit nutty and what part is an expression
of a deep, dawning anxiety. The letter snaps back into focus
when Salinger expresses this anxiety directly: How afraid he is
of losing Lobrano, how he would not be able to write for *The
New Yorker* anymore without Lobrano as editor. He discusses
his fondness for William Maxwell and then says he couldn't
write for Maxwell because he once went to a movie with Maxwell called *The White Mane* that Maxwell and his wife liked,
and Salinger thought a piece of trash. This is followed by a lament on the horrors of ego. And then a rather stunning evocation of Salinger himself as grief stricken and at a loss — he has
been writing letter upon letter to Lobrano but then tearing
them up. What right does he have to send letters to a sick person? he asks. Then he imagines Lobrano in Nassau, in a glass-
bottomed boat[2] and wearing a seersucker suit,[3] and the fantasy

---

2 Lobrano liked to fish, and took his writers fishing. Perhaps this was behind
the fanciful, leisurely image of a man in a glass-bottomed boat, but the image
also feels terribly poignant when I consider that it was Lobrano's edit of "A Perfect Day for Bananafish" that launched Salinger at *The New Yorker,* and in this
image Salinger seems to be wishing for many happy returns to the world of
Bananafish for them both. But it was not to be.

3 This seemed like an arbitrary image until I learned, to my amazement, that
Lobrano had grown up in New Orleans and graduated from the Isidore New-
man School, located about eight blocks from where I live.

assuages him for a moment. But then the anxiety returns, and he continues to go on for two more single-spaced pages on the subject of Zen.

Dorothy has been reading the letters to me on the phone in a rather deadpan voice, low and a bit scratchy. It feels very intense and old-fashioned, like someone calling in copy to a newsroom.

"He goes on for two more pages about Zen," she says after a moment.

"What does he say in those two pages?" I ask.

I can hear her handling the pages — the sound of hesitation.

"It's about how Daddy should take responsibility for his body, and do this and that," she says.

I can sense her skimming the pages. She reads a line out loud, Salinger imploring Lobrano to see his body as a perfect expression of God . . . and if he does it with enough force . . .

Dorothy's voice trails off.

I am quiet for a moment. This passage in Salinger's letter is shocking. What Salinger wrote in the earlier part of the letter, about phlebitis, about his need and respect for Lobrano's editing, about the glass-bottomed boat, was so warm, so charming, so recognizably and uniquely J.D. Salinger. This was something else. Every negative feeling I have ever had about the cultish assurance of the religious comes to the surface.

"The Zen stuff is . . ." I begin.

"Almost cruel," says Dorothy.

Yet in spite of those two pages the prevailing mood of the letter is one of love. Salinger was, at the time, a famous author with a wife and a baby. He was pretty well situated in his own adulthood. Yet his voice, here, has the tremulousness of a child contemplating the loss of someone he loves.

She next read me a letter from 1954, a year after Salinger had attended the wedding of Lobrano's son, Ducky, to a woman named Sandy. Salinger was writing about his own recent elopement with Claire Douglas.

Dorothy starts reading without the salutation. I have no idea what, if anything, she is leaving out. Salinger writes of his perverse wish to be blasé and undramatic about the news, as though he were reporting a minor cold, and then announces that he and Claire have eloped. He says he is very happy but then adds that he wishes he could react to it in a Ducky-and-Sandy sort of way. He tells Lobrano that this is the first letter he has written on the subject. (I flash to the exchange he had with another beneficent parental figure, Elizabeth Murray, when breaking the news of his first marriage to Sylvia.) He then speaks of Lobrano as the person who most understands his own difficulty in letting things go, who understands the meaning of restraint. It seems he means this editorially — finishing stories — but it's ambiguous.

"What does he mean, 'Sandy-Ducky sort of way'?" I ask Dorothy.

"I think he just couldn't handle happiness," she says. "Or telling people he was happy."

When I ask for her opinion about his use of the word "restraint," she points out that after her father stopped editing Salinger, "All forms of restraint went out the window. Or at least quite a bit of it."

This brings us back to that other letter, which Salinger wrote when her father was in the hospital, just before he died.

"That Zen stuff is just hectoring," I say.

" 'You have got to make yourself better,' " she says. "Kind of insensitive. We didn't show it to my father, he was so sick at that point."

The last letter she reads me is the earliest. It is dated January 29, 1951, and was sent from Westport, Connecticut. "He seems to be answering a letter in which Daddy turned down a story."

She reads me the passage alluding to the rejection. The letter then turns grateful, as though Lobrano had instructed him on the crucial difference between creativity and novelty, between writing that is challenging and writing that is rigid in its refusal to accommodate the reader. Salinger says he is putting the story away, and though he will probably make the same mistakes, he hopes it will not be for a long while.

The letter then swerves to recall the work Lobrano did on "A Perfect Day for Bananafish," specifically a query Lobrano made about a line of dialogue. Salinger had defended the line on the grounds that it was essential to Seymour Glass not sounding too flippant and Lobrano agreed. Salinger mentions this, he explains, because this sort of granular scrutiny of his stories was something he did back then — all of three years earlier — but had drifted from now, and he wanted to regain that focus, patience, and discipline as quickly as possible. He says he has a story in mind that he is going to start work on right away. And then he talks about children in his fiction, and how he should give them a break and stop demanding they come down from their tree house because the only way to do it is to wait for them to come down on their own.

After that, Dorothy and I get off the phone.

"Raise High the Roof Beam, Carpenters" was the last story by Salinger that Lobrano edited, though Dorothy thinks her father may have seen drafts of "Zooey." Nevertheless, when *The New Yorker* considered J.D. Salinger's "Zooey" for publication, Lobrano was no longer alive. The fiction department turned it down. William Shawn overruled them. After that, Salinger was edited exclusively by Shawn.

It is difficult to begin talking about William Shawn. Saying he was an incredibly talented editor seems insufficient. He was surrounded by a secretive aura that seemed preoccupied with manners, decorum, and discretion. He was physically small and, in the realm of American literary culture, a giant. To compliment him is an almost impossible act—it takes a genius of Salinger's stature to pull it off, in the dedication of *Franny and Zooey,* where the praise is so ostentatious it teeters perfectly between sincerity and self-mockery.

Shawn took a successful, influential magazine and elevated it to another level of commercial success (money is always clarifying), while at the same time considerably broadening its scope. It had been a humor magazine with in-depth reporting. It became a magazine that handled much more serious material at length, without losing its sense of humor. The fiction department, meanwhile, only grew in stature. As Roger Angell, who ran the fiction department for many years, put it, *The New Yorker*'s fiction "was like the major leagues."

Another problem with discussing William Shawn is that he was a bundle of odd neuroses and I'm anxious about listing them, lest they turn this formidable figure into a cartoon.

Some minor oddities: He always carried an umbrella. His workdays were punctuated by cornflakes for lunch at the Algonquin. Small, bald, withheld, whispery. Sufficiently paranoid about elevators and the prospect of getting stuck in one that *The New Yorker*'s office building had a manned elevator devoted almost entirely to his use. The office legend was that he carried a hatchet in his briefcase in the event the elevator got stuck, almost certainly a joke, but resonant.

Medium-size oddities: Although he was the father of three children, he was averse to bodily functions and sex being represented in any way in the magazine and also in conversation. In *Here at The New Yorker,* author Brendan Gill included a famous anecdote involving Gill and Shawn at lunch with the English novelist Henry Green. Shawn asks what inspired him to write his novel *Loving.* Green's reply includes the now legendary remark about the pleasures of "lying in bed on Sunday morning, eating tea and toast with cunty fingers." The anecdote has the resonance of myth because of Shawn's subsequent blush and Green's obliviousness to his infraction. Harold Ross used profane language but kept it out of the magazine. Shawn simply did not use that kind of language, and neither did anyone else while in his presence.

Major oddity: This most chaste figure was revealed to have conducted a decades-long affair with staff writer Lillian Ross (no relation to Harold), a revelation provided after his death by Ross in her 1998 memoir of the relationship, *Here but Not Here.* Shawn lived with his wife and two sons but would usually make time in the evening, after dinner, to leave his home and stroll down the avenue to visit Lillian Ross and the son she adopted in the mid-1960s, a son he apparently treated as his own.

Lillian Ross has written profiles of cultural figures for *The New Yorker,* with a focus on show business, since 1945. She is still alive and is a regular contributor to *The New Yorker.* Her most famous piece was a long profile of Ernest Hemingway. She has a sharp eye, a knack for animating scenes and for revealing people through their conversation. I want to say that her abilities of self-perception are strangely limited, but that is just too much of an understatement, given the aura of discretion that surrounded William Shawn — an aura dispelled by the details of his relationship with Lillian Ross.

Here but Not Here, published six years after William Shawn's death but while his wife was still alive, reads like it was written in a trance. It's an expression of a kind of romantic post-traumatic stress disorder. The portrait is of a man who is happily in love with a woman. That the man just happens to have a wife and children with whom he is concurrently living is treated as an inconvenience transcended by the power of their love. Shawn comes off as a kind of Madison Avenue bigamist.

In *Here but Not Here* any feelings of resentment, dissatisfaction, jealousy, and anger have been repressed, with the predictable result that they manage to find expression anyway. The scandal makes a mockery of all the discretion and whisperings, and at the same time, denuded of the myth, one can see that Shawn's light footsteps were in the service of an important idea: Writers are not patients in a hospital, but they do need quiet to concentrate. They need privacy.

There was something about the aura of Shawn and his ethos that suggested that publishing was a vulgarity and possibly damaging to a writer, an odd position to take for someone in charge of a weekly magazine, publishing tens of thousands of words in every issue. But that was the message that was gradually absorbed into the culture of *The New Yorker* under William Shawn.

Salinger had been focused on the destructive effects of publication before Shawn became his editor. He rushed off to Scotland when *Catcher* was published. He took his photograph off the back cover once the book's success granted him the authority to do so (it was there for the first two editions; by the third edition it was gone). He wasn't a privacy neophyte. But Shawn's obsession with privacy dovetailed with Salinger's. Lobrano's editing seemed always to turn Salinger's work toward the real world, the concrete world. The concerns of the reader were front and center. They went back and forth on "Franny," for example, to address the concern that readers might think Franny was pregnant; Salinger wrote a line trying to directly refute this misunderstanding: "A long time between drinks" (too opaque, people thought she was pregnant anyway). Perhaps because of fear of offending Salinger, Shawn seems to have been less demanding. Conversely, in her book *Gone: The Last Days of The New Yorker,* Renata Adler reports that Salinger said he didn't want to show Shawn his new work for fear of offending him with its sexual content.

I don't think Salinger's course was going to be set by any other lights than his own by the time Shawn became his editor.

But I can't resist wondering how things would have proceeded had Gus Lobrano lived.

I asked someone who had been close to Shawn to talk to me about J.D. Salinger. The response was silence. Then I got a note from this person declining to participate in my book, but going on to reflect on Salinger's silence and its influences. The letter, filled with interesting observations that were off the record, was wrapped in a veil of secrecy within which was a case for the value of secrecy to the creative act. It was not there, but there: "I do share the quasi-superstitious feelings that were so much a part of the old *New Yorker* attitude: don't talk about things you plan to write about, or you may not be able to write about them. Writing is a mysterious ceremony whose secrets must not be disclosed to anyone."

35

1960s–1980s: Letters to the Swami

THE MORGAN LIBRARY now holds three folders of Salinger letters. Two of them are recent acquisitions. The announcement of Salinger's correspondence with Marjorie Sheard made the front page of the *New York Times*. The one announced just two weeks prior generated much less press. It was Salinger's correspondence with Swami Nikhilananda, the founder and spiritual leader of the Ramakrishna-Vivekananda Center of New York, who had brought Vedanta Buddhism to the West as a disciple of Sri Sarada Devi. Reading Salinger's correspondence with the Swami, I was confronted by my various ambivalences and even antipathy to the role of Zen Buddhism in his life and work.

There were sixty sheets of paper in the Swami folder. The tone of the letters is different from all other letters Salinger wrote. Some of this is because the Salinger correspondence I am most familiar with was written by a man just out of his teens to his early thirties. In the letters to the Swami we are in the middle of that vast empty space of the third panel of the Salinger triptych, which happens to be Salinger's middle age.

But like a parent—a mother, to be honest—who simply cannot assimilate the culpability of her child when confronted with the evidence (that he is a pot smoker, that he is a thief, that he has failed all his classes), I look for the corrupting influence so I can lay blame somewhere besides on the beloved.

It's almost as though the case against Zen being a constructive force in Salinger's work — as opposed to, say, his myth — can be found in this folder of letters to the Swami. They lack the irreverence that makes his other letters so enjoyable. Absent are the strange leaps into Marx Brothers nonsense and illogic; absent are the absurd, bizarre digressions and impersonations.

Salinger often signed his letters with a fake name. "Fitz Dudley" was a personal favorite. None of the letters to the Swami is signed with a fake name. They are respectful and even warm, but they lack the intimacy of the warmth he once exuded so easily in his writing. One of the fascinating things about Salinger's epistolary style is the confidence with which he conducted himself, his graciousness and good manners enhancing the sense of being genuine as opposed to impeding it, as forms sometimes do.

There was something about the distance implicit in a letter that allowed him to come forth with genuine warmth. The letters to the Swami gesture in the direction of warmth, they even strain for it, but the respect with which he is writing quashes any feeling of a personal connection. Well, I suppose one is not chummy with one's guru. Also, part of this awkwardness may have had to do with a semiconscious awareness that English was not the Swami's first language. At any rate, the first letters in the folder did not really entertain in the way almost every other Salinger letter does.

But then after ten or so letters, which often involve references to a new book by the Swami that has either been sent to Salinger as a gift, or that Salinger discusses purchasing — he seems to buy multiple copies with the idea of some low-level proselytizing — I got to the notes that had been typed out to accompany his donations.

In 1974, Salinger sent a check for $500, made out to the Ramakrishna-Vivekananda Center. The letter that accompanies his check is a brief note saying that he hopes that it will help defray expenses at the center. This brief, formal note nevertheless contains more personality than all the previous correspondence. There was something intensely familiar about it, even familial, but I couldn't locate what it was until I turned the page. There I found another letter, also typed, brief, and delivering the same message as the previous one, in almost the exact same words. He was sending a check for $500 to help defray the expenses incurred by the center and in the hope that it would help the center do its valuable work. The first letter was from 1974 and the next one was dated 1975. When I turned the page and got to 1976, and read the note that said the same, with perhaps one tiny variation of phrasing, since, after all, each year he typed a new note, I suddenly figured out what I recognized in these brief notes: Salinger was accessing his inner grandparent. He was very good on the speech rhythms of little kids, and he was also very good with old people, the two most notable old people being a professor at the start of *The Catcher in the Rye* and Holden's grandfather, with whom he rides the bus. But those passages had been impersonations, performances as William Maxwell put it, and these notes are the real thing. Page after page, year after year, Salinger makes his sincere and well-meaning donation of $500 and accompanies it with a note. The length and phrasing fluctuate; some are briefer than others, none more than a few sentences. The size of the check, like the song, stays the same.

At some point, when the dateline of the letters was in the mid-1980s, I started to laugh. I started to picture the Swami, and the people he worked with at the center, as having those same extremely un-Zen feelings I once had when receiving a check from my grandmother. The exasperation wasn't so much about the sum, which in my case was usually $50. The problem with the grandparents' monetary gift is that the grandparents do not adjust for inflation — inflation in the sense of cost of living, but also inflation in the literal sense: The recipient is getting bigger. His needs are growing concurrently.

Salinger starts out with $500, a very generous sum, and from his point of view its value surely goes beyond what $500 can buy in any given year, beyond the sense of emotional support and gratitude and endorsement such a gift carries — from the grandparents' view, which is the long view, the value is that it is there every year. Implicit in the size of the gift and its constancy is a little lecture on the value of prudence, frugality, saving for the future, a future in which, precisely because of these virtues, the grandparents may have some money left over to give you another check. But the grandchild can't really imbibe this on an emotional level even if he understands it intellectually. The recipient of the gift eventually starts to lament the fact that it never gets bigger. What started out as a gift and an acknowledgment of the recipient's existence — *you are there, grandchild, I care about you; here is money, use it well, but it's yours however you want to use it* — becomes something that signals almost the opposite — *here is money, the same money for the same person who is not the same, and if I could see I would see the person was not the same, the world has changed, the person has changed . . . here is more money!*

Year after year, page after page, $500 checks come with the accompanying typed letters, and finally, at last, in 1996, more than two decades since the first check, the sum increases to $1,000. This is the only check that has been photocopied and included in the file.

The real news at the Morgan Library, for me, was not in the correspondence with the Swami or even the young fan, interesting as those were, but in the letters Salinger wrote over a period of forty years to Michael Mitchell, an artist friend he made when living in Westport who had done the artwork for *The Catcher in the Rye* cover. What is fascinating about these letters is that they persist, and with genuine warmth, to a much later date than the other letters Salinger wrote to Elizabeth Murray and Whit Burnett. He had a falling-out with both of them: in Murray's case because after their correspondence had dwindled she sold his letters; with Burnett because of a publishing dispute in the late 1940s.

In these letters to Mitchell we hear an intimate voice into the 1980s, decades past the last time we heard his voice on the printed page. The note of fatigue and despair and sheer crotchetiness is stronger here. At one point he alludes to the "shitty literary kids." I found this shocking, not so much for the language or even the sentiment exactly — a similar group of poseurs is alluded to in the letters to Marjorie Sheard — but because of the way he sounded so worn down by the battle with these "shitty literary kids," with their pretensions to scholarship, which Salinger felt was just gossip dressed up in tweed. The army of woodchucks had been assaulting his garden for a quarter century by then. A garden he tended so carefully, out of the deepest sense of spiritual need and artistic imperative. The possibility of his not having engaged in the war against these "kids" does not occur to him. Strangely, it is exactly at the moment when the cost of the war in spirit is most evident that I sort of see his point — fuck the woodchucks! It's his life and his property, intellectual and literal. No matter the cost-benefit analysis of guarding every leaf against intrusion, it is a matter of principle. A principle I was, of course, violating at that very moment, leafing through his intimate, private musings with my own shitty literary justification that they are an important part of Salinger's literary expression.

The Catcher in the Rye: Rereading and Birthing

THERE COMES A point when focusing on J.D. Salinger for long enough, as an adult, you start to be drawn back into the person you were when you first read him. In my case, and I suspect the case for many people, that person may have been having some troubles dealing with the world, their responsibilities, school, life. Everyone has trouble dealing with these things, always, but especially in junior high and high school. For some people the difficulties are mostly internal, for others they come spilling out. In my own experience, the catastrophes large and small from this era undergo a strange transmogrification at some point in your twenties, when they are far enough away. They become a strange source of pride. In the case of my own expulsion from high school, it has slowly become a badge of honor.

Whereas I once regarded being thrown out as a source of shame, I am now rather proud of it. I felt an element of pride at the time, too, but mostly I was afraid that the school administrators' message, their comments about me, would be the final word; that they would be right about my being, in essence, wrong.

But now I know they were wrong, or at least not predictive. My pride in the matter has been burnished, if not outright invented, by the reactions that people have to this fact. Over the years, what people say when it comes out that I was thrown out of high school is some variation of "Cool!"

Then they want to know why. There are two answers to why someone gets thrown out of school. One involves what exactly he or she did to so anger the administration. The other is much more complicated, psychological, and individual, and is not something you could, or should, chat about casually. Anyway, it's not what is being asked for. One answer is an anecdote. The other is a novel, maybe a novel like *The Catcher in the Rye.*

Coming back to the work of Salinger as an adult, especially an adult with children, my perspective on it all is much different: I see Holden and the other characters. I see Salinger himself as I study his life and work. They are players on a field. To some extent I see myself, too. The fat, fatherless, fucked-up, angry, cowardly, lonely, socially awkward, needy, mother-attached, underachieving, wise-ass eighth grader who so annoyed Mr. Colan and all the other teachers — someone told me that the French teacher I had in seventh grade had a nervous breakdown because of me. Probably not true. Though we corresponded decades later, by e-mail — a brief, polite exchange that he initiated (still teaching French at that school, restored, apparently) — during which I felt, within the back-and-forth, a cathartic note on his part, as though this was a final putting to rest of some troubling episode I might have instigated or played some role in.

But all this perspective starts to collapse after a period of being immersed in Salinger. The distance. The sense of bemusement. After a while a kind of emotional vertigo occurs and you start to enter the point of view of that kid, that reader of *The Catcher in the Rye.* And a terrible, trembling fear comes over me, a fear I thought I would only experience at this point in my life for the people I love — my wife, my children, my mother. But this is different. It's not even self-pity, or not only self-pity. It's self-recognition, connecting with the neediness of that boy reading that book, among others, and starting to find my way toward language as some kind of catharsis.

Salinger would sometimes check into hotel rooms in order to write — a process he once referred to as "getting it out of me." He was engaged in a process that was cathartic and maybe even exciting — a reconnection with the old fears combined with, perhaps, some of the new adult-writer fears that he might not, in fact, be able to get it out of him. To think of it that way makes it sound like a birth. Like Holden has been in him all this time, and forming all this time, and now it is time to get him out, to take him out, and let him be autonomous and breathe the air everyone else breathes, for better and for worse. I think of that phrase of Burnett's, reflecting on that period over two semesters — Salinger sitting in the back of his class smoking and looking out the window, only to come forth at the very end with "very edited material." Interestingly, Salinger often wrote of how much he loved his own writing as he was writing it, but then later couldn't stand to look back at it.

Now I have scampered back to my Olympian perch, looking at the panorama of Salinger's life and work. But it's a scary thing to slip back into the old self. The kid you were. I think of Salinger working and reworking the Holden character and related characters in those many stories he was writing during the 1940s. Shaping him up, fleshing him out. You give birth to a baby; Holden is a young man in *Catcher.* A baby is born. A kid like Holden, half a head of gray hair already and a smoker's cough, does not get born — he escapes. Like a jailbreak. Which, if you put it that way, makes Salinger himself the jail from which he needed release.

Acknowledgments

I would like to thank the following people and institutions for their generosity and support: James Atlas and Mary Evans, editor and agent, without whom this book would not have been started or finished, Dorothy Lobrano Guth, Sarah Norris and Dr. Margaret Norris, Whitney Burnett, Adrian Benepe, Joanna Scharf, Bob Strauss of Camp Wigwam, Princeton University's Firestone Library, Tulane University and its Howard-Tilton Memorial Library, the Harry Ransom Center at the University of Texas at Austin, the Rare Books and Manuscripts Room and the New York Public Library and its staff, Michael Congdon, Penelope Green, Rich Cohen, Alan Zeigler, Richard Locke, Judi Roaman, Kenny Karlstein, Hava Beller, Liselotte Stern, Donald Meyers, Adam Casdin, Genie Everett McClosky, Ben Yagoda, Thomas Kunkel, Brian Koppelman, Scott Smith, the Morgan Library, Louise Mirriam, Louis Menand, Sasha Weiss, D.T. Max, John Seabrook, Radhika Jones, Bill Buford, Shelley Wanger, Roger Bellin, Scott Oldenburg, Nick Peruffo, Michael Hoffmann, Deborah Garrison, Phillip Lopate, Maggie Sivon, Ed Park, and especially Jonathan Ames. Most of all my wife, Elizabeth Beller, for the support that spans the logistical, emotional, intellectual, into realms unfathomable and delightful.